ISBN-13:
978-1500687557

ISBN-10:
1500687553

THE ART OF MARS

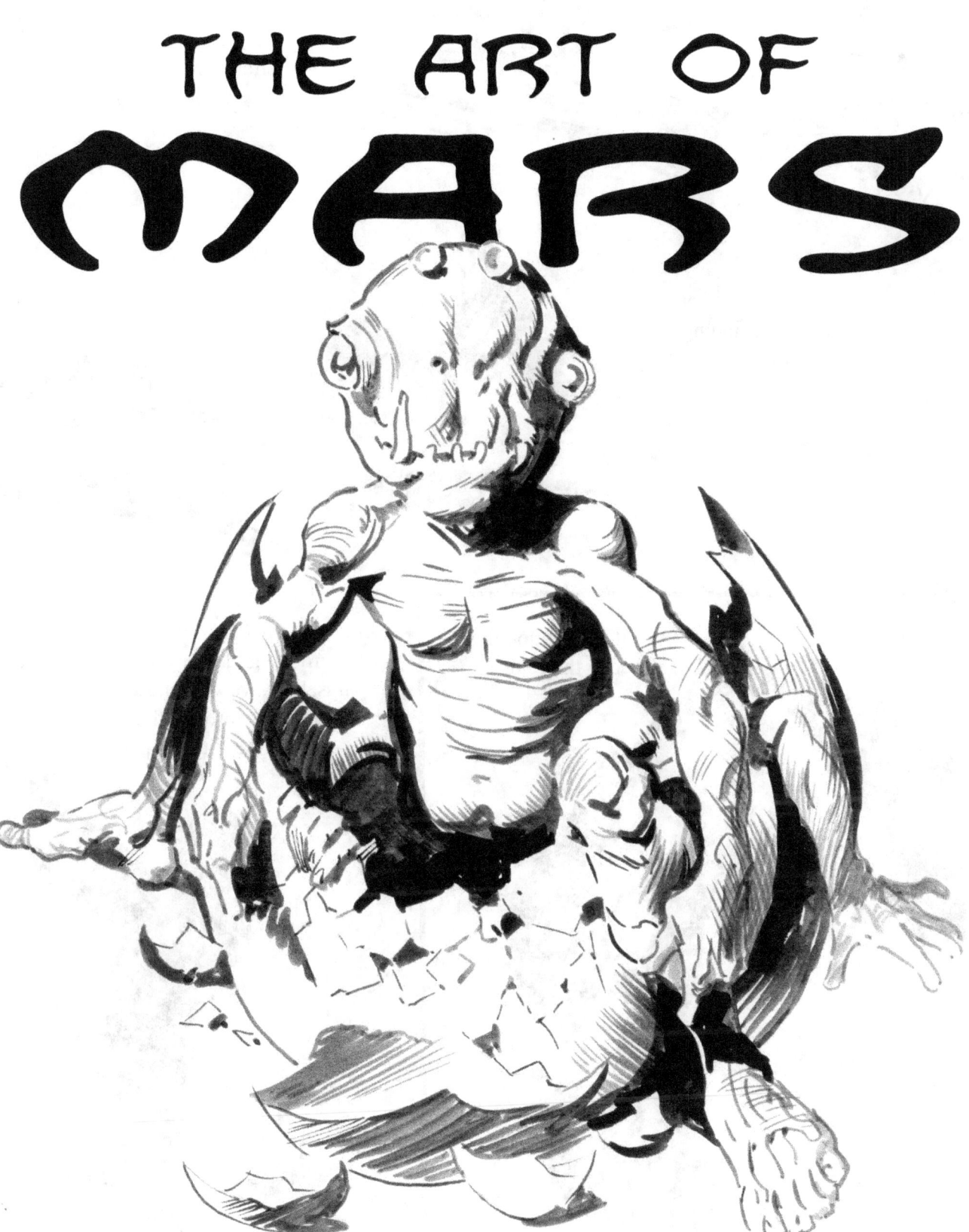

ILLUSTRATIONS BY MIKE HOFFMAN FROM THE FIRST THREE
"MARS" NOVELS OF EDGAR RICE BURROUGHS

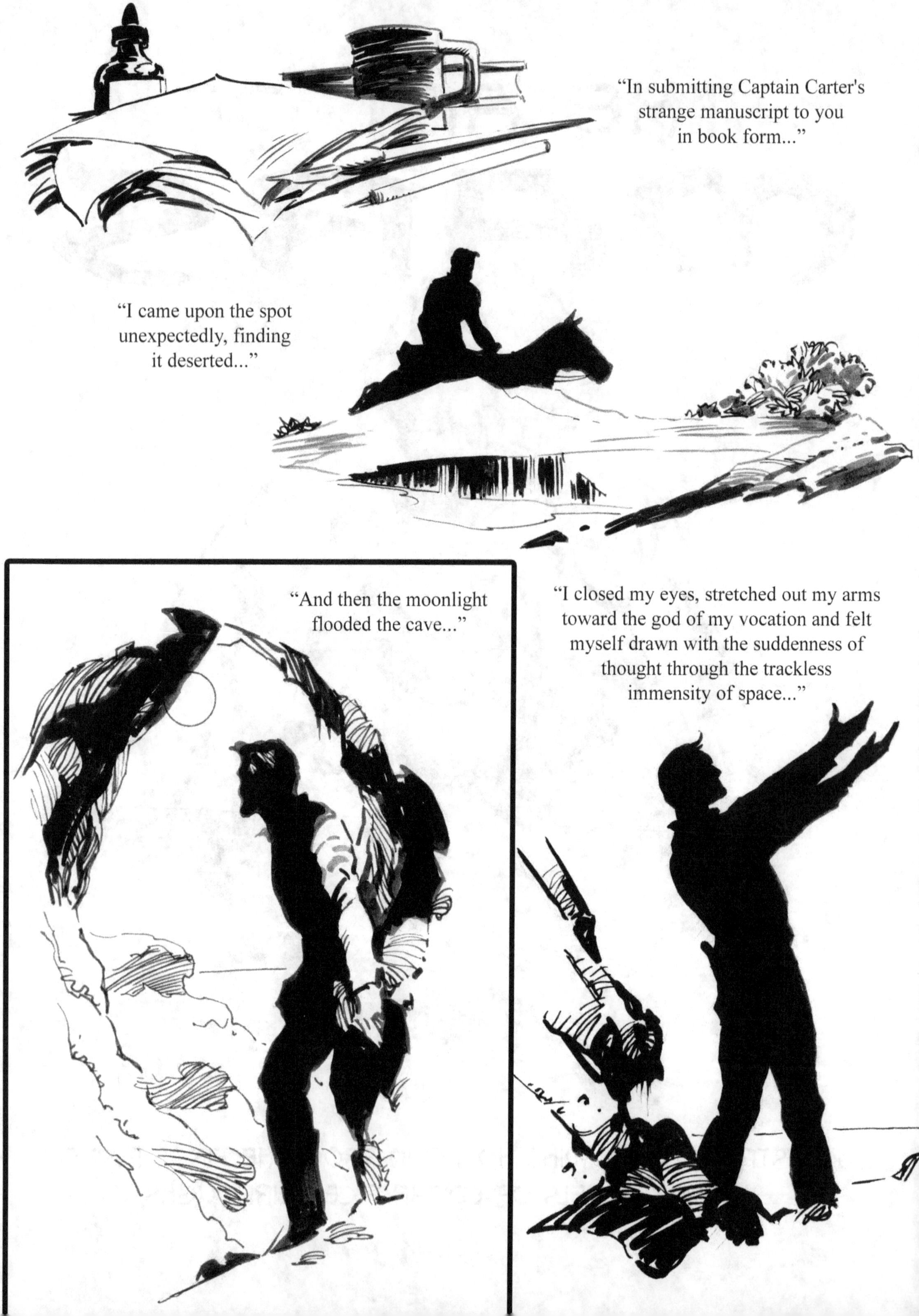

"In submitting Captain Carter's strange manuscript to you in book form..."

"I came upon the spot unexpectedly, finding it deserted..."

"And then the moonlight flooded the cave..."

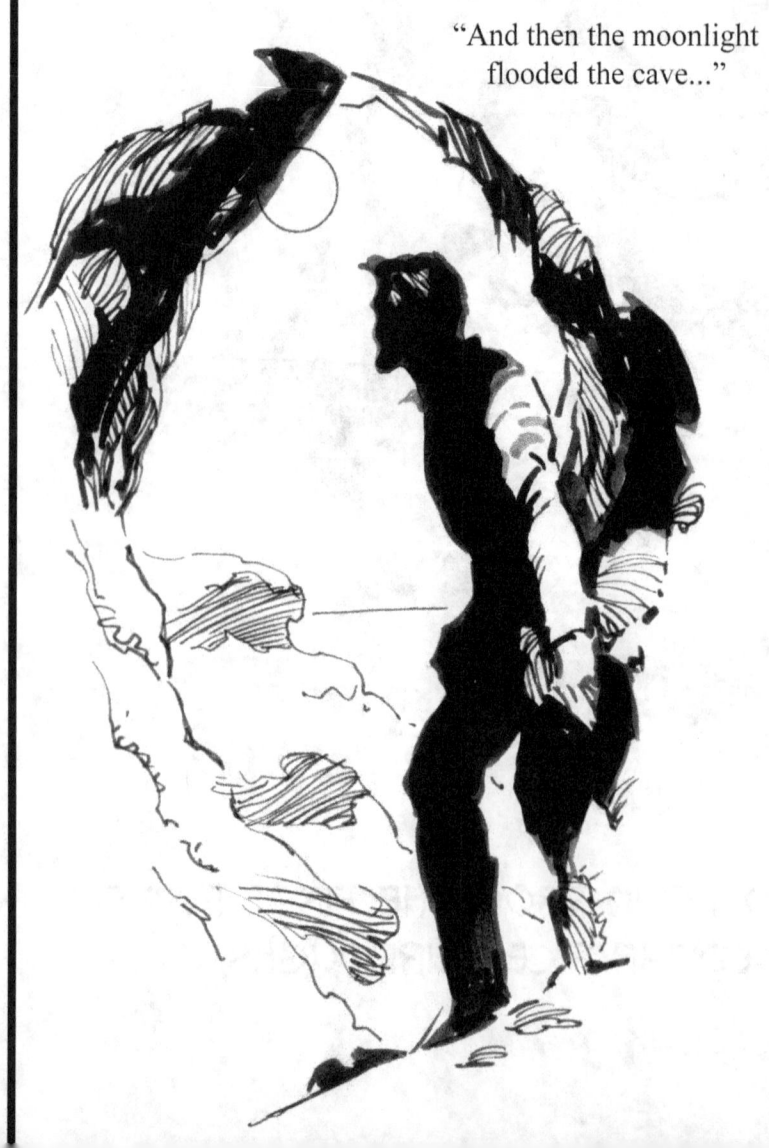

"I closed my eyes, stretched out my arms toward the god of my vocation and felt myself drawn with the suddenness of thought through the trackless immensity of space..."

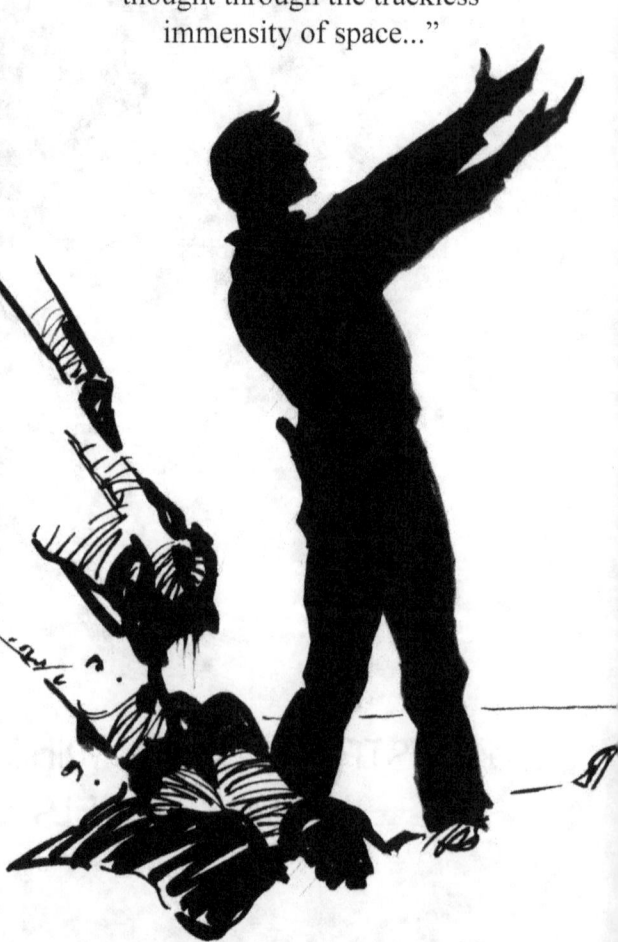

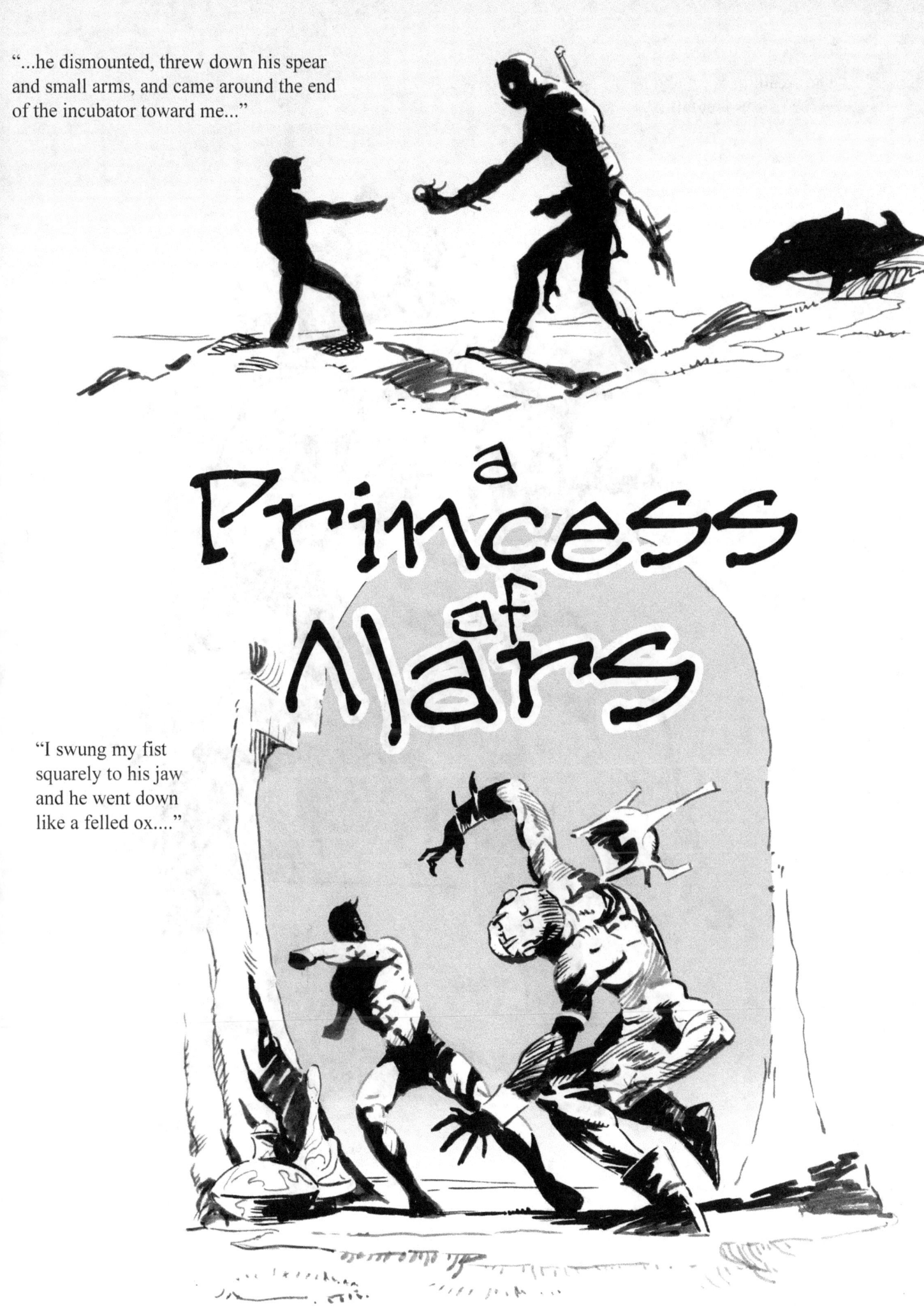

"...he dismounted, threw down his spear and small arms, and came around the end of the incubator toward me..."

a Princess of Mars

"I swung my fist squarely to his jaw and he went down like a felled ox...."

"The creatures were about ten
or fifteen feet tall..."

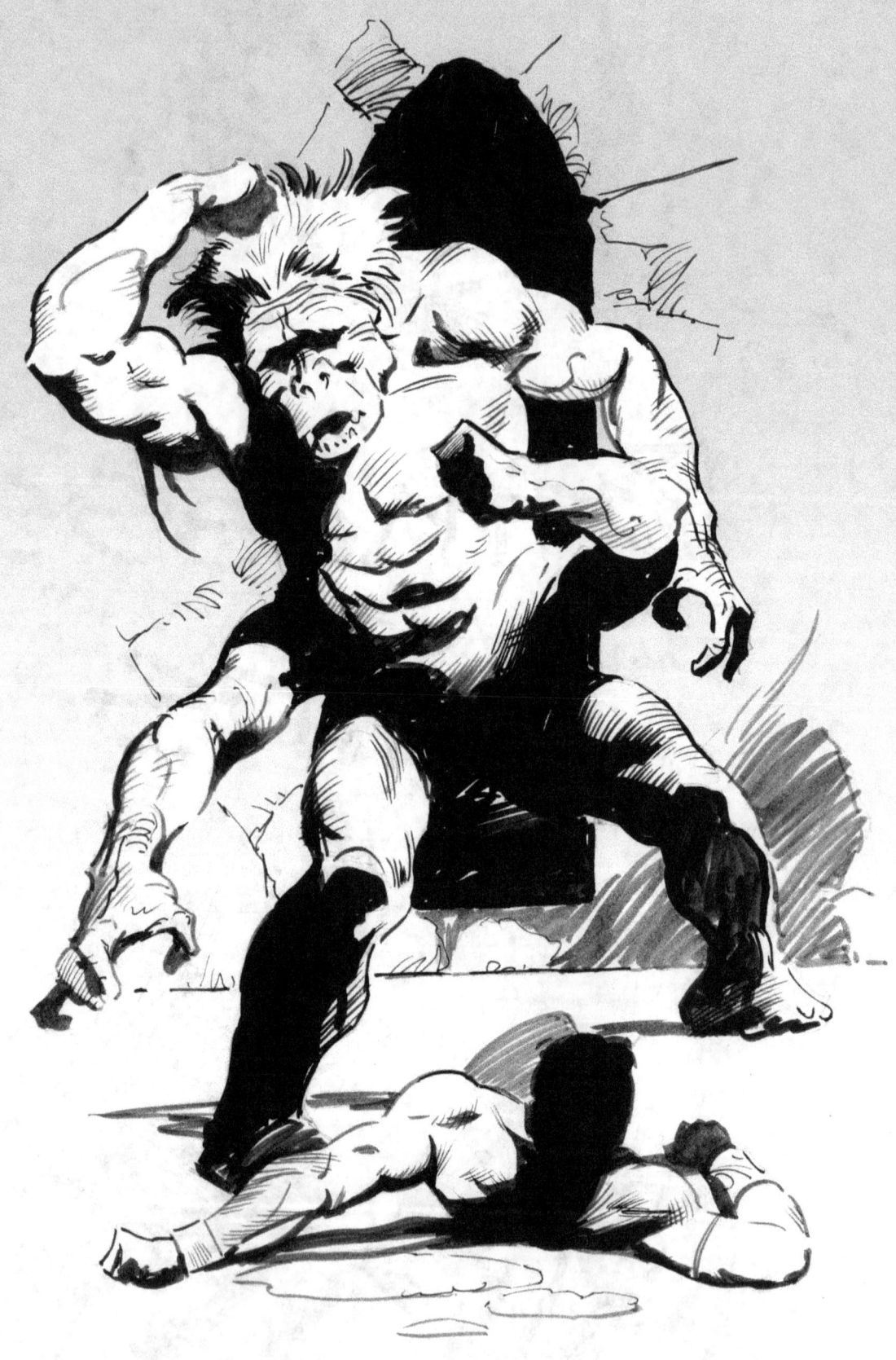

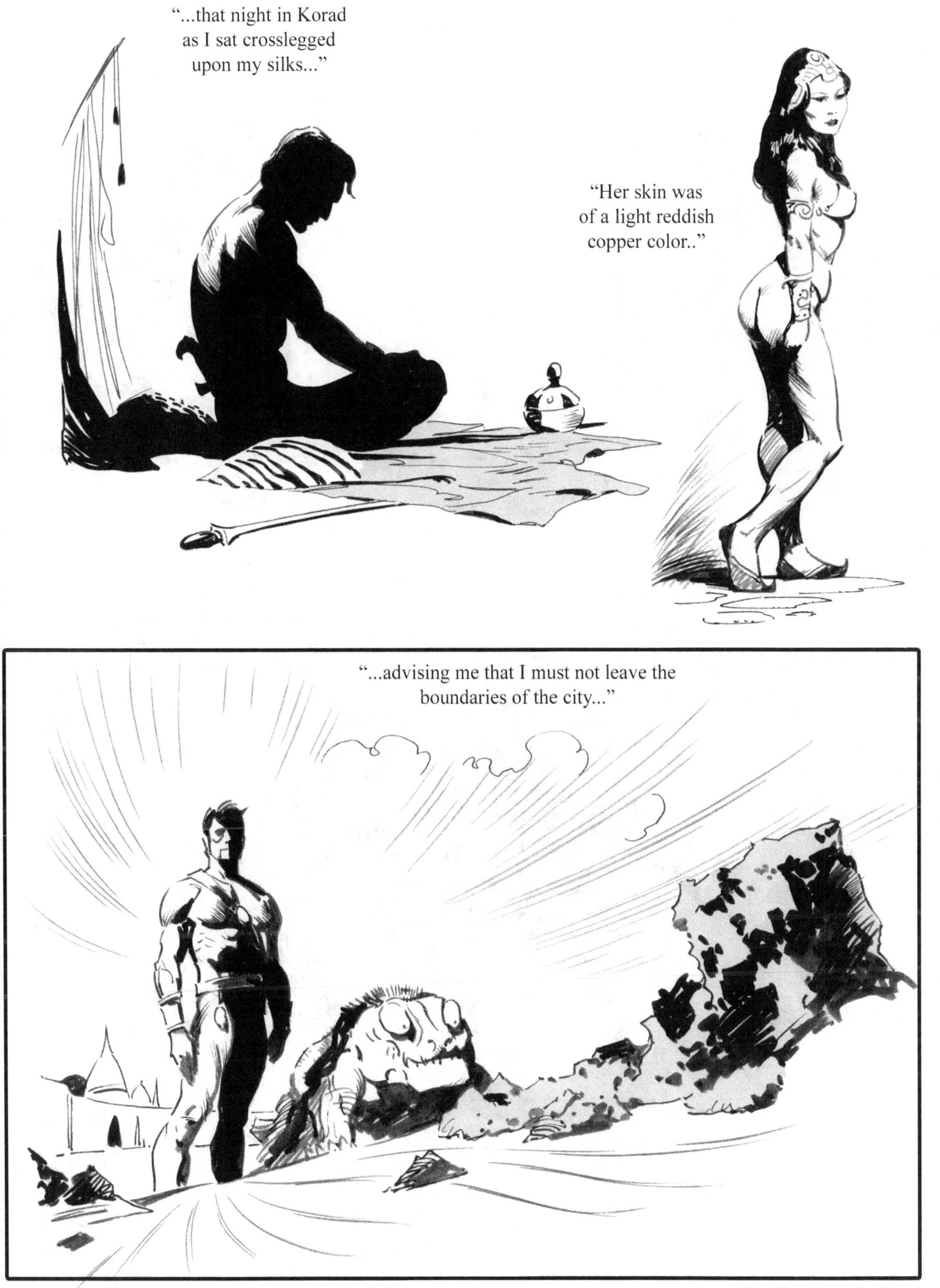

"...that night in Korad
as I sat crosslegged
upon my silks..."

"Her skin was
of a light reddish
copper color.."

"...advising me that I must not leave the
boundaries of the city..."

"...the captive Martian girl."

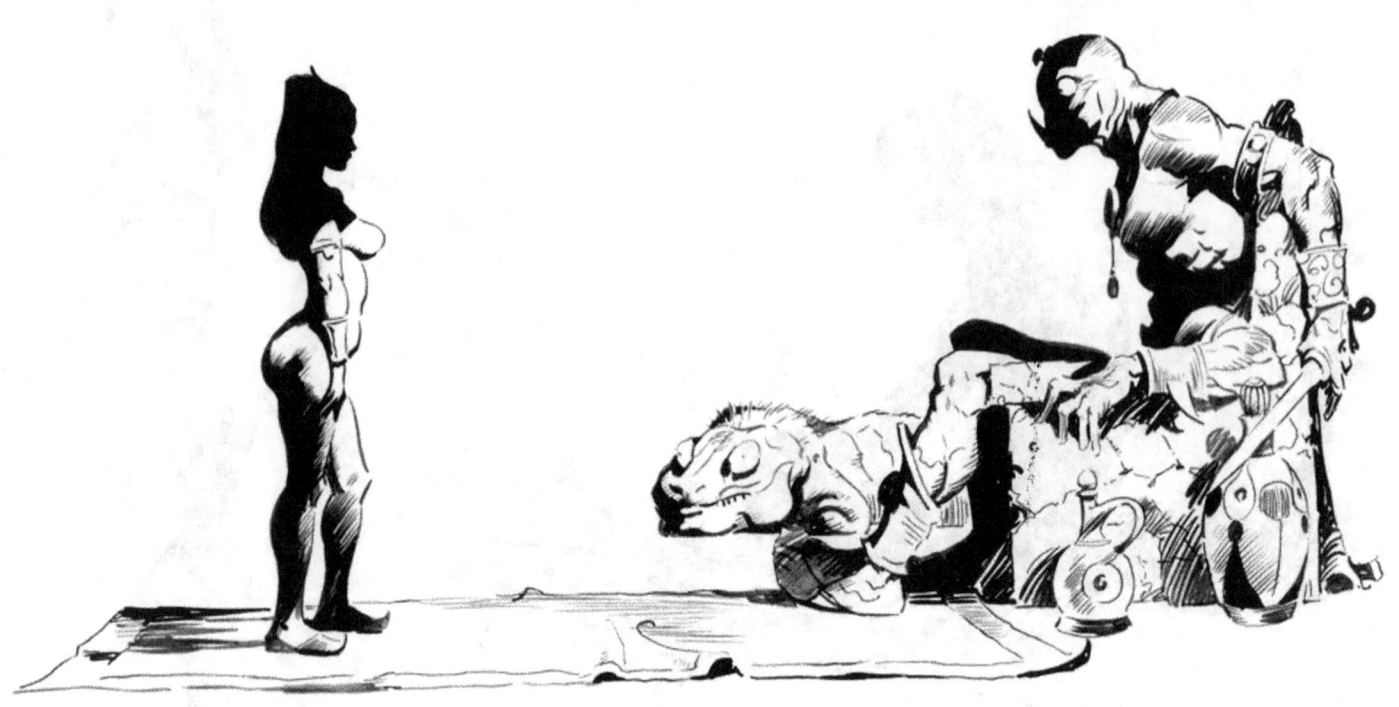

"Zad first attempted to rush me down
as a bull might a wolf, but I was
much too quick for him..."

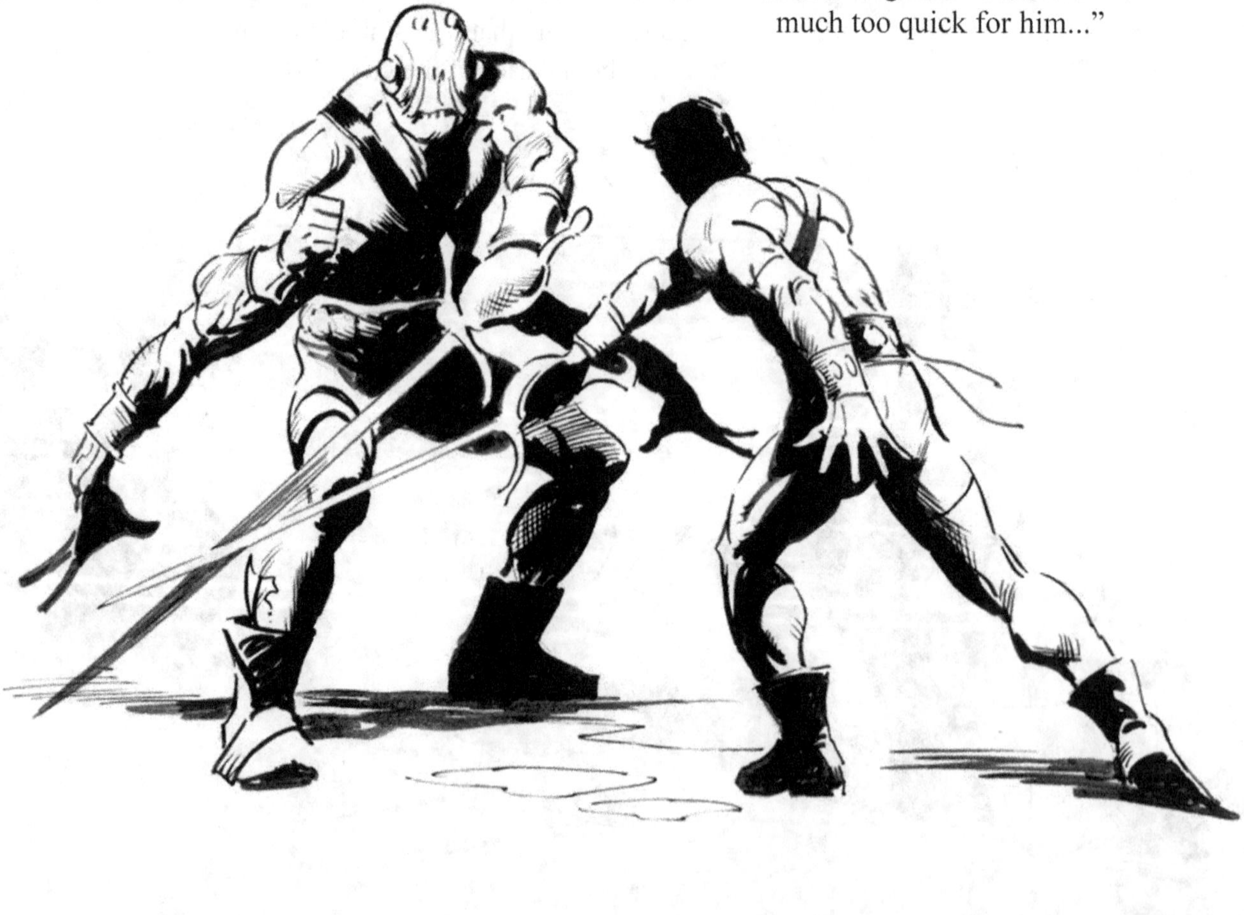

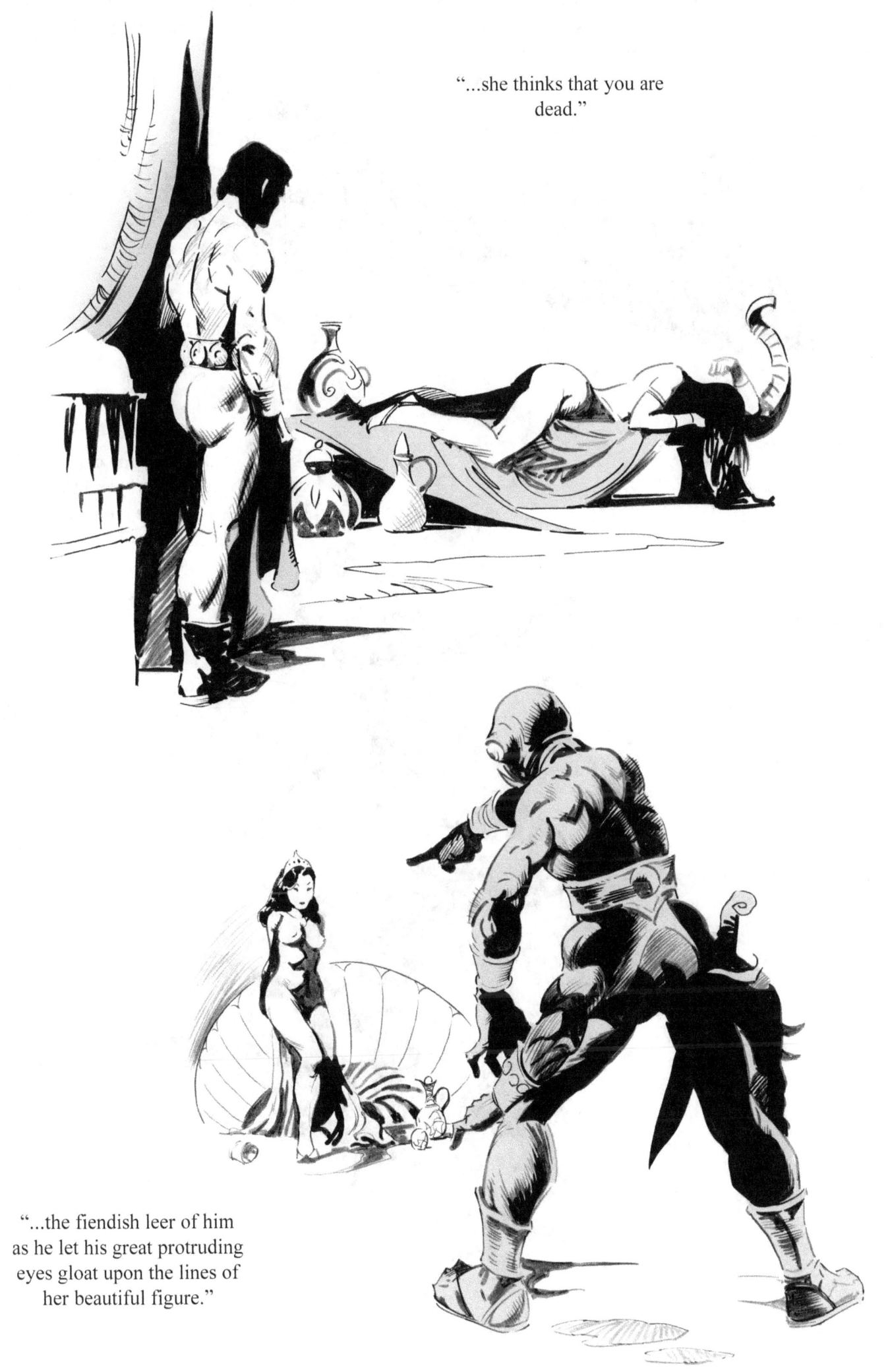

"...she thinks that you are dead."

"...the fiendish leer of him as he let his great protruding eyes gloat upon the lines of her beautiful figure."

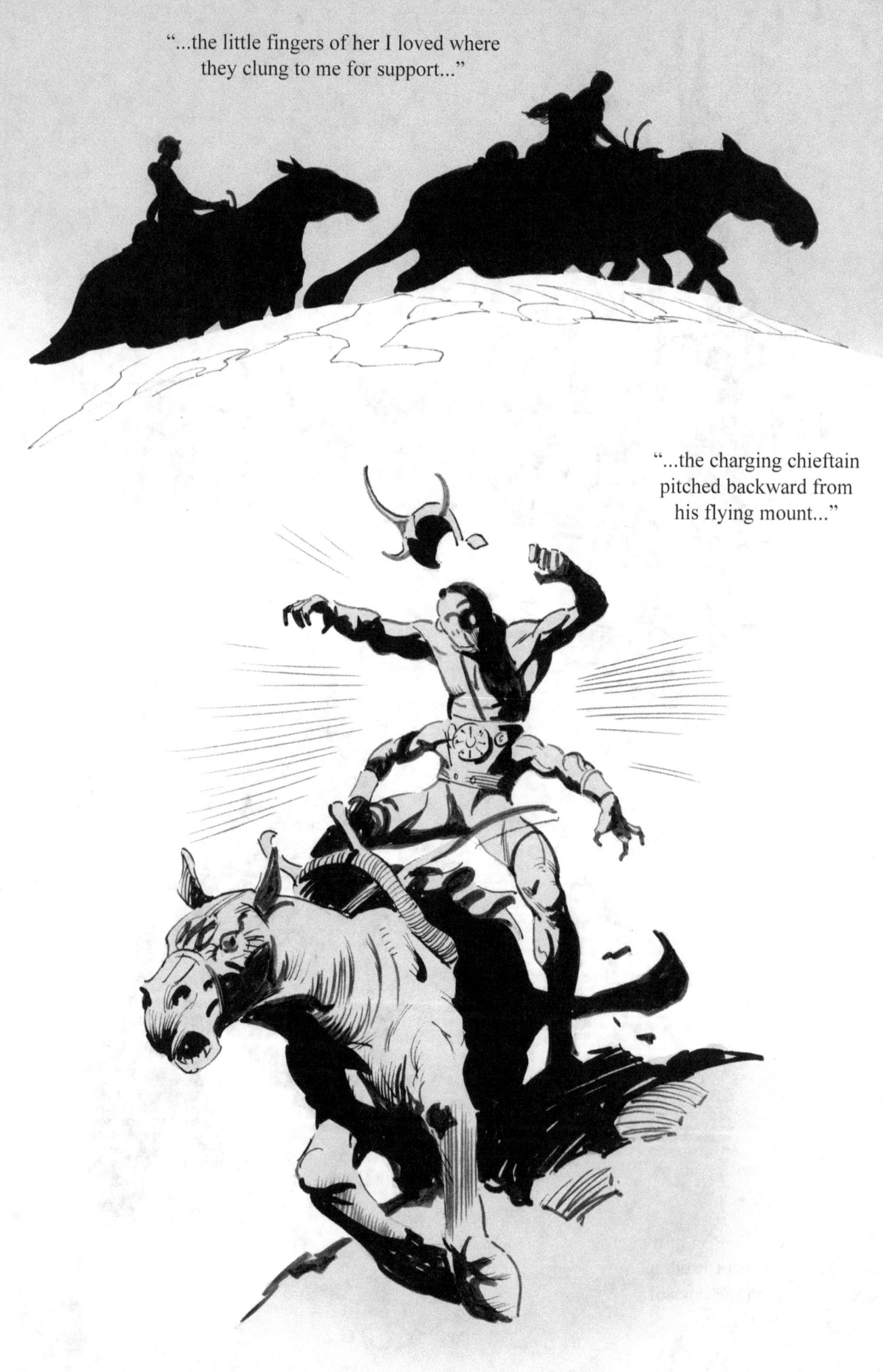

"...the little fingers of her I loved where they clung to me for support..."

"...the charging chieftain pitched backward from his flying mount..."

"The dead jeddak's hands and head were removed to be added to the ornaments of his conqueror..."

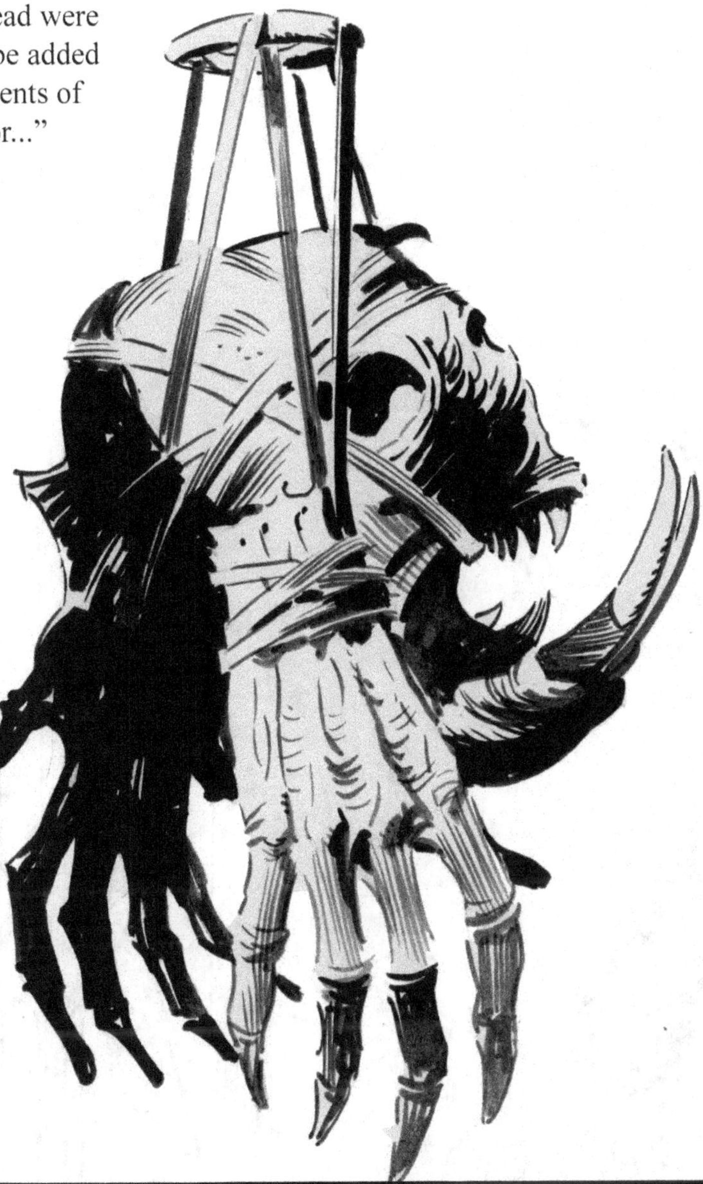

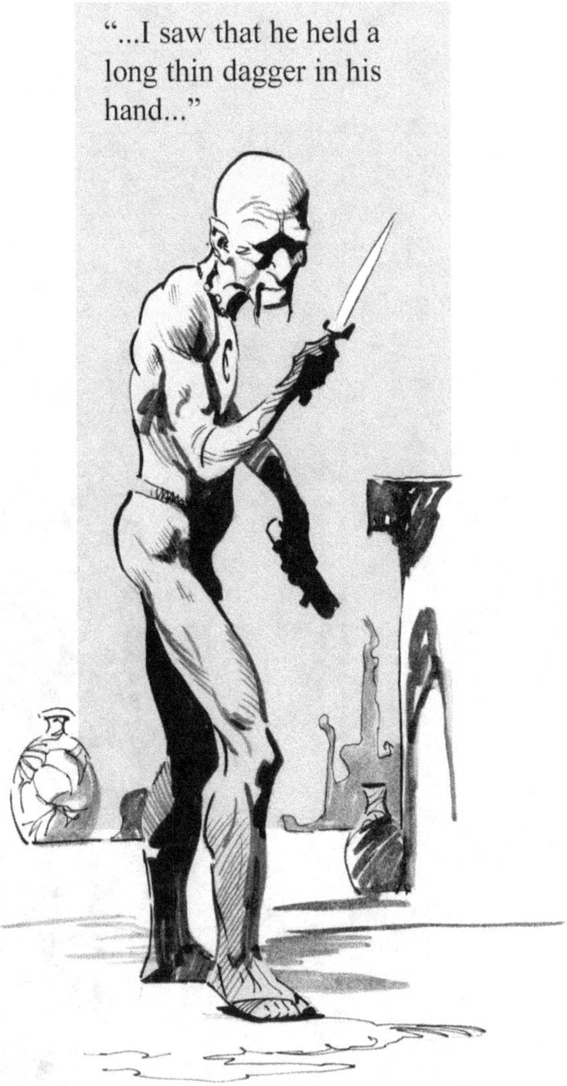

"...I saw that he held a long thin dagger in his hand..."

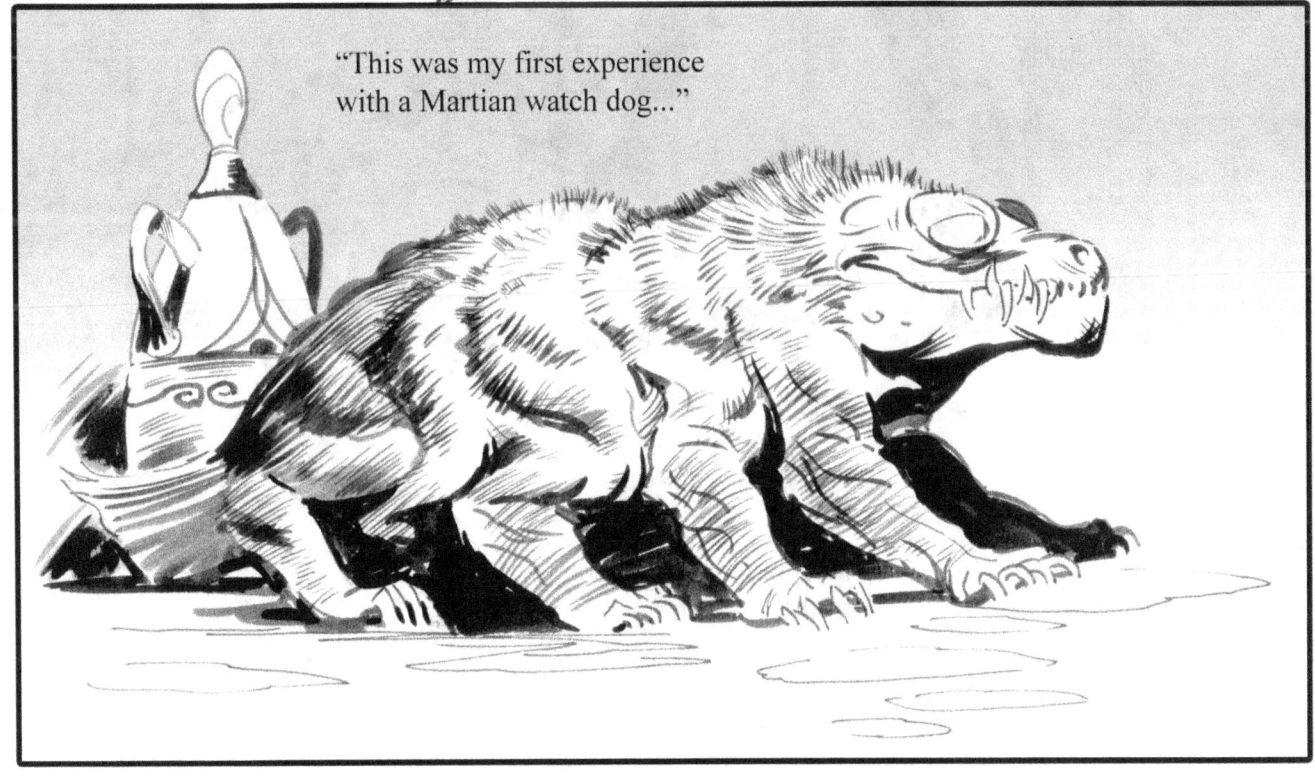

"This was my first experience with a Martian watch dog..."

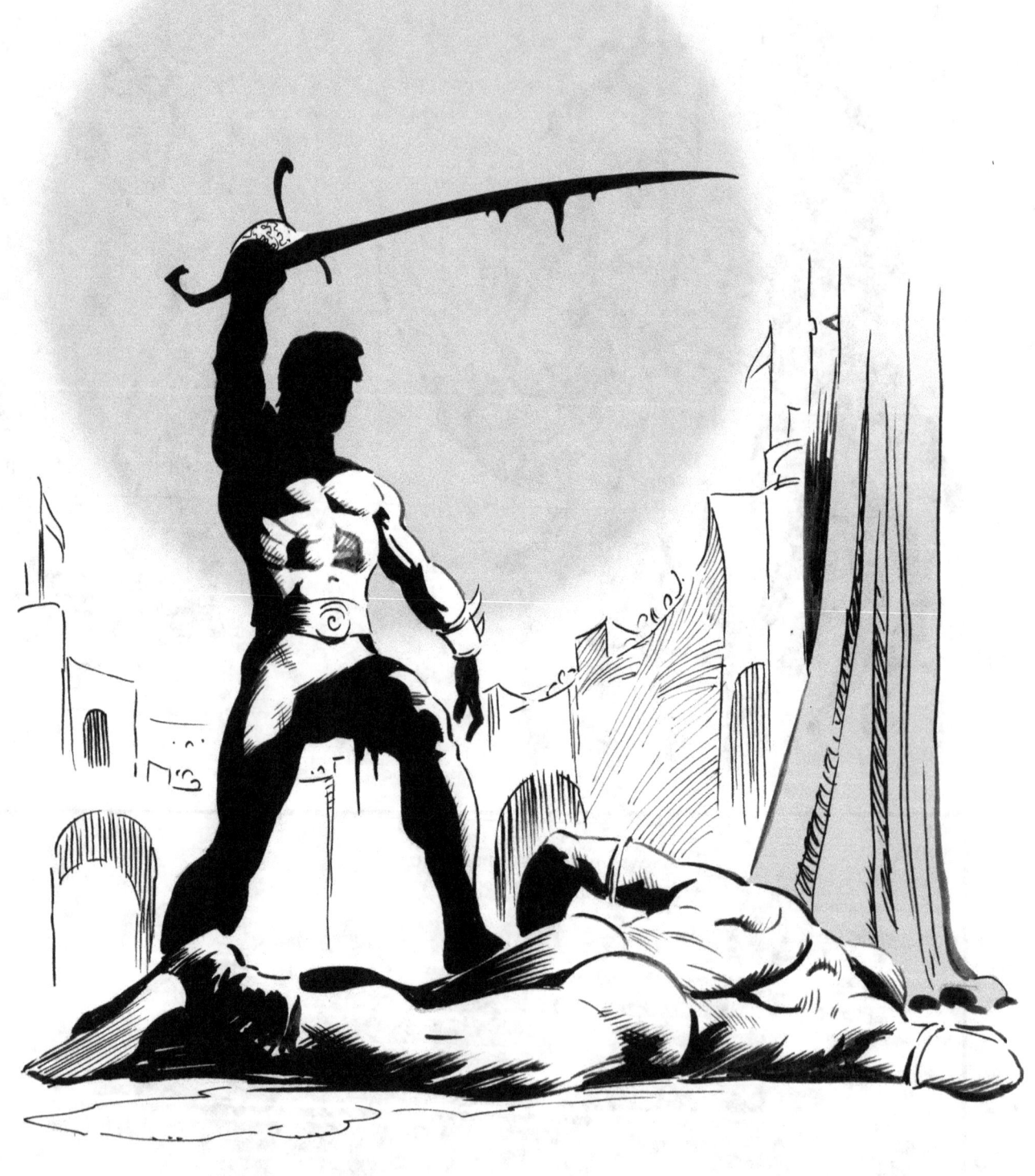

"Time and time again I won the applause
of the bloodthirsty multitude..."

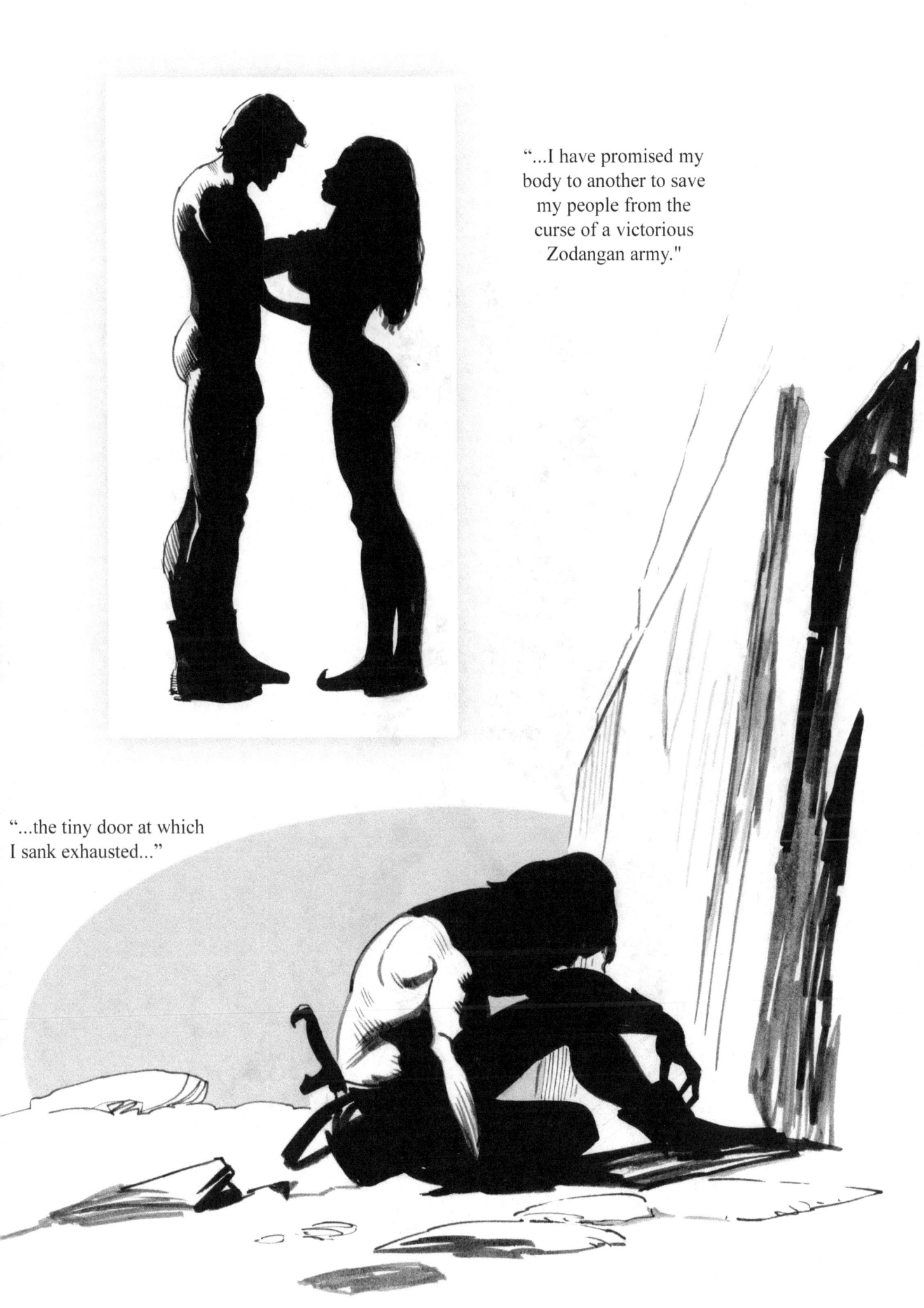

"...I have promised my body to another to save my people from the curse of a victorious Zodangan army."

"...the tiny door at which I sank exhausted..."

"'Strap him to that
pillar,' he shrieked."

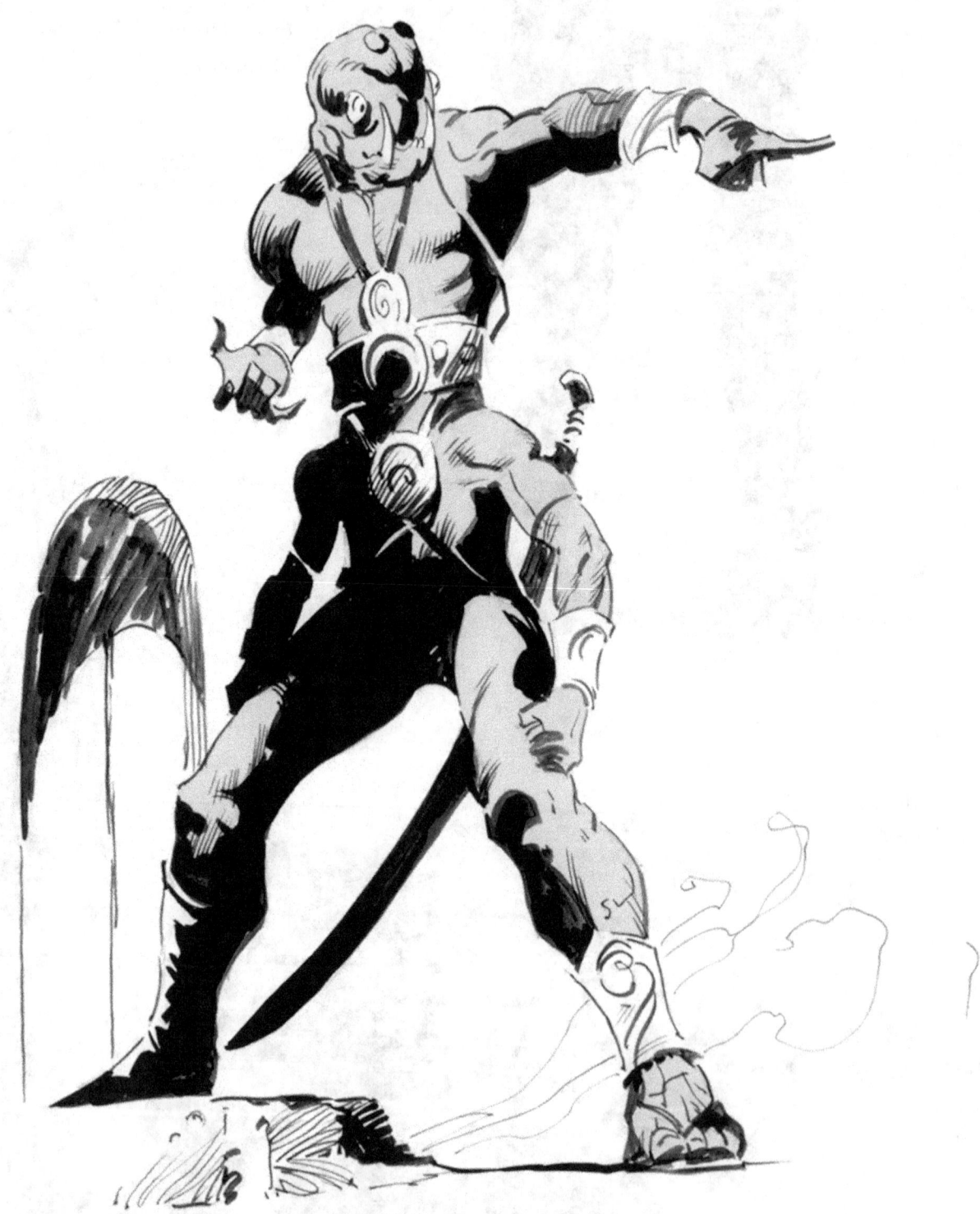

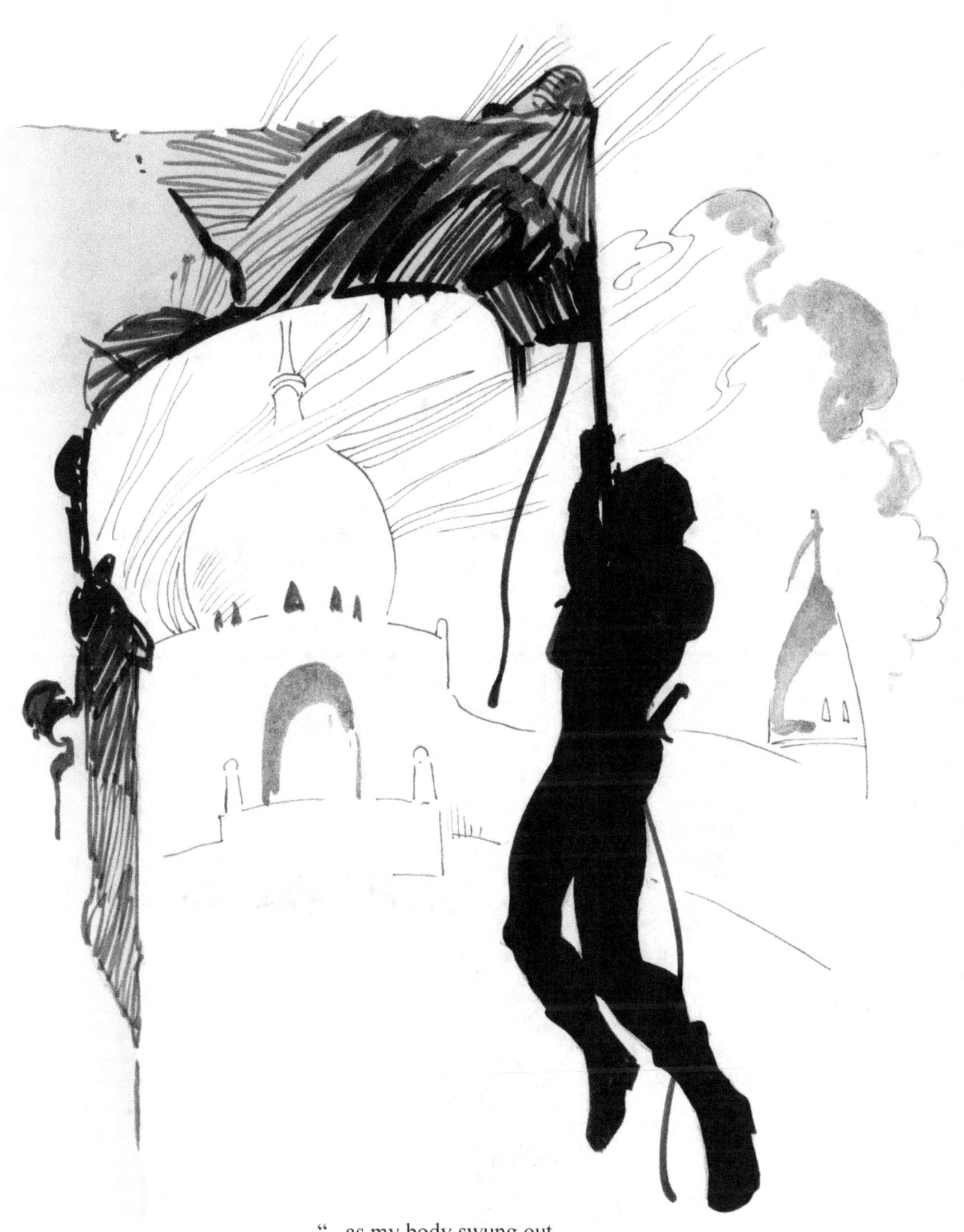

"...as my body swung out
at the end of the strap it would
slip off and launch me to the
pavement a thousand feet below."

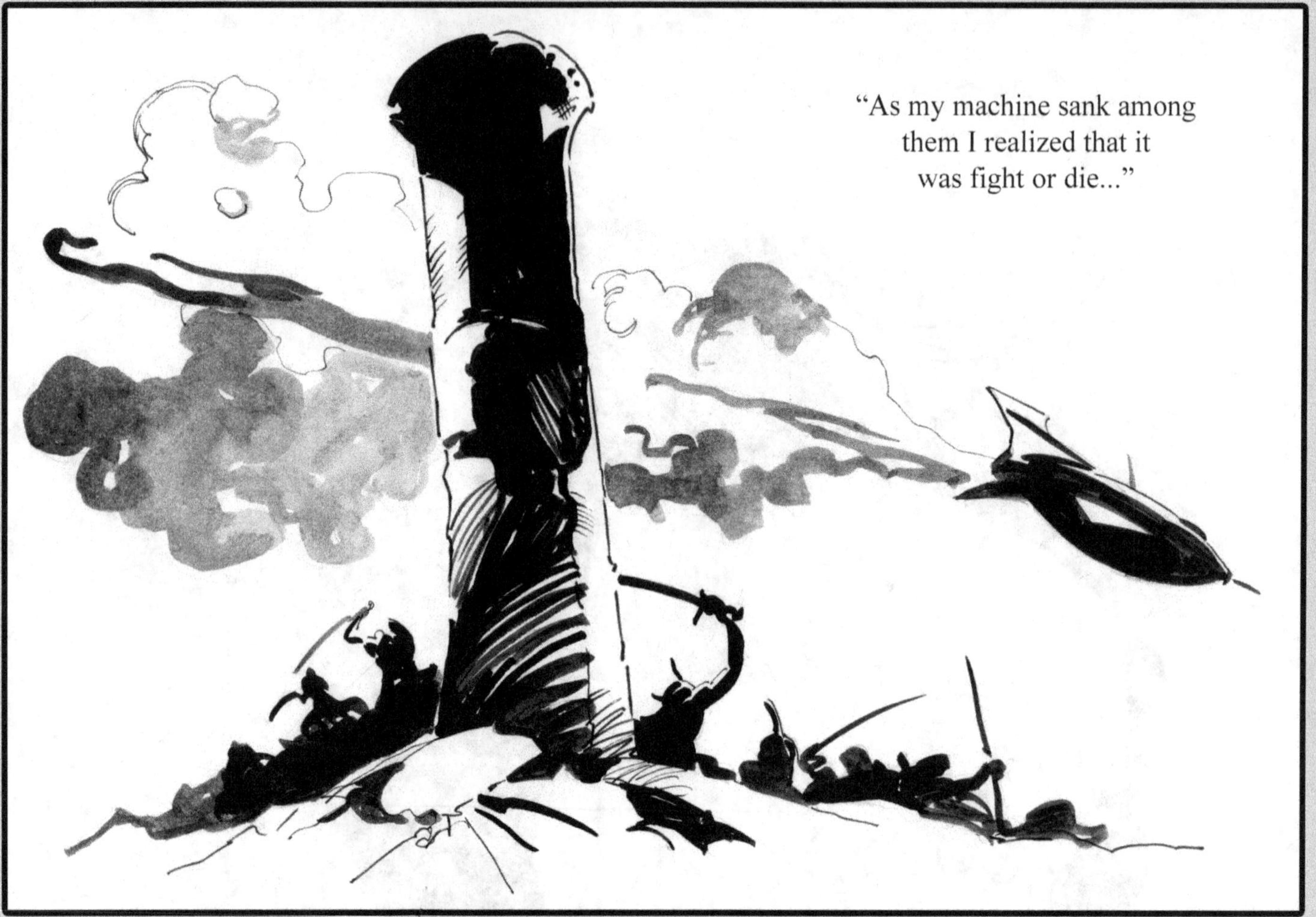

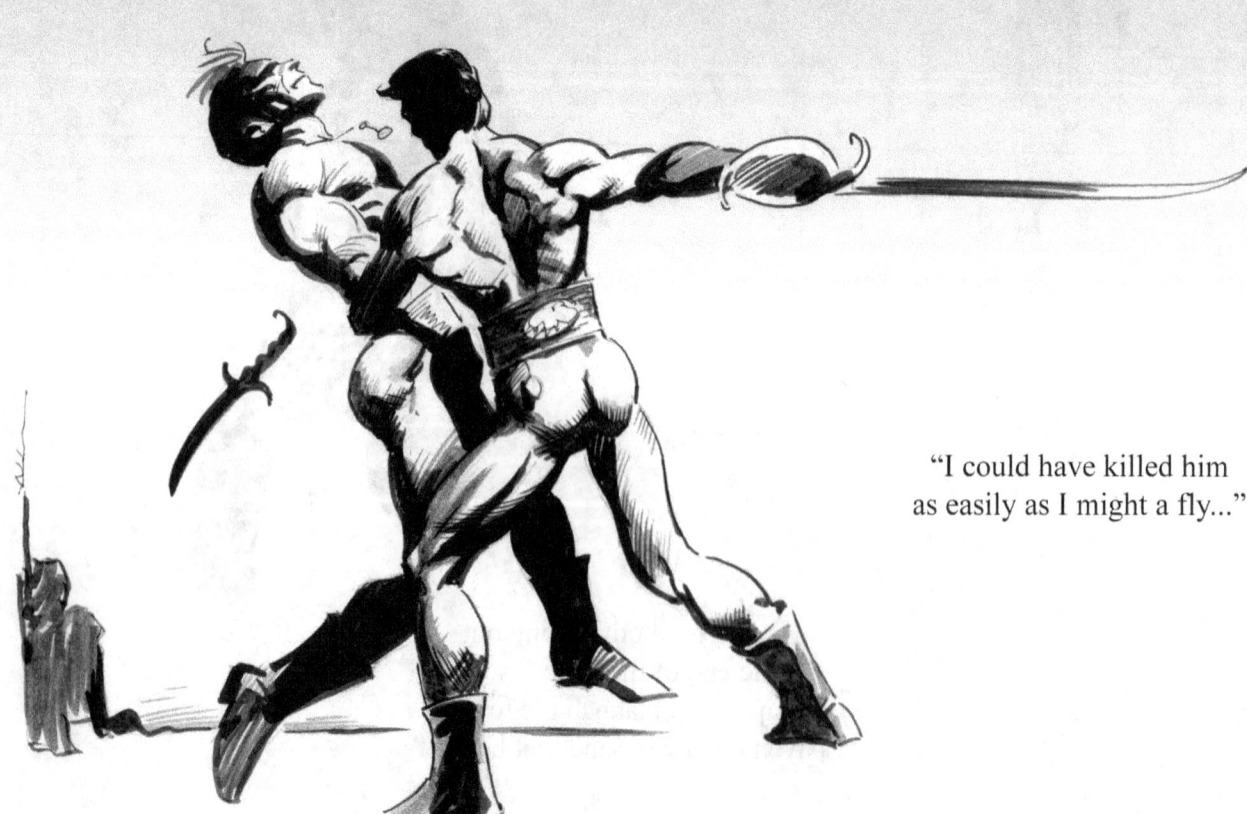

"As my machine sank among them I realized that it was fight or die..."

"I could have killed him as easily as I might a fly..."

"...the more
I begged her to
explain the more
positive became her
denials of my
request..."

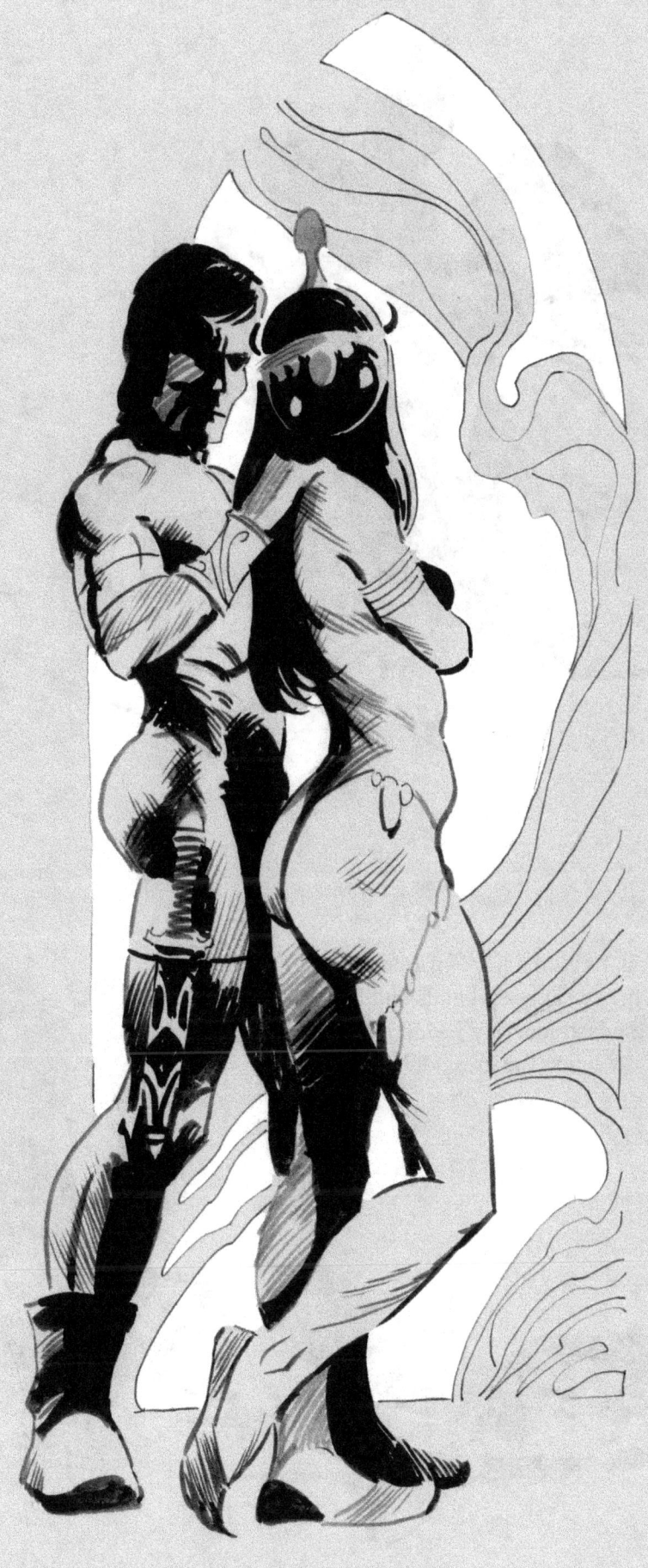

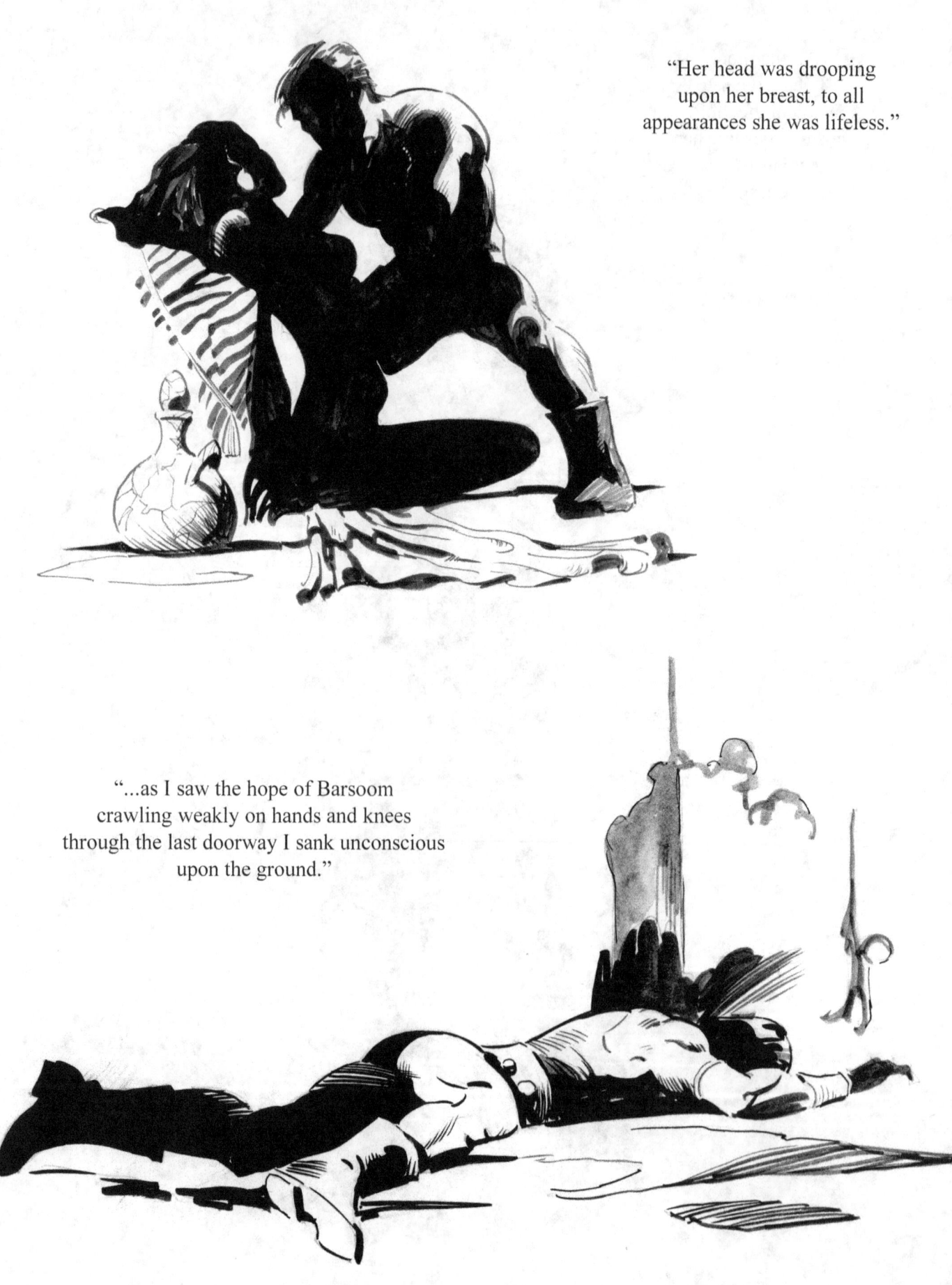

"Her head was drooping upon her breast, to all appearances she was lifeless."

"...as I saw the hope of Barsoom crawling weakly on hands and knees through the last doorway I sank unconscious upon the ground."

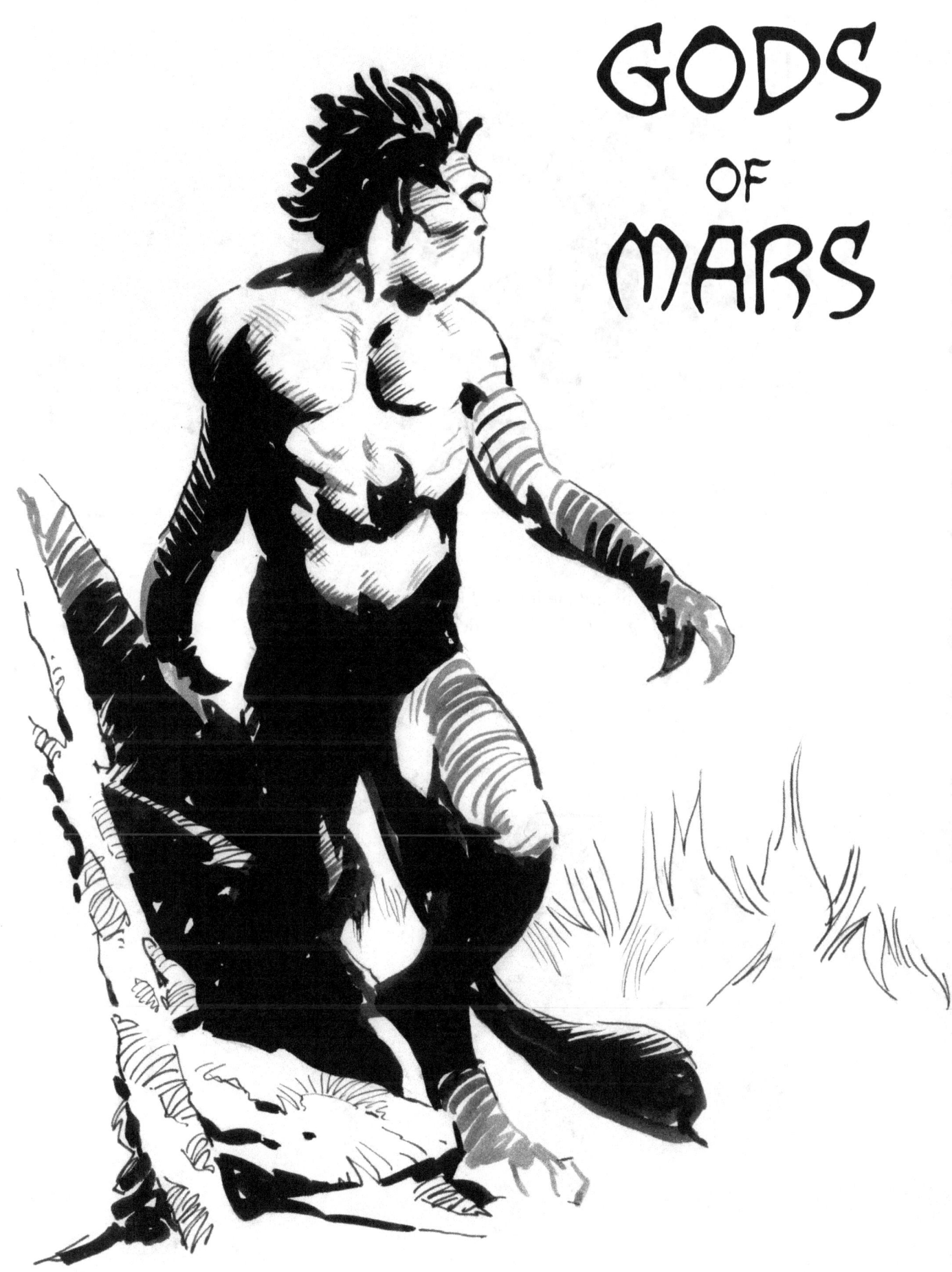

GODS
OF
MARS

"The fastest flier of the Heliumetic Navy could not quickly enough have carried me far from this hideous creature."

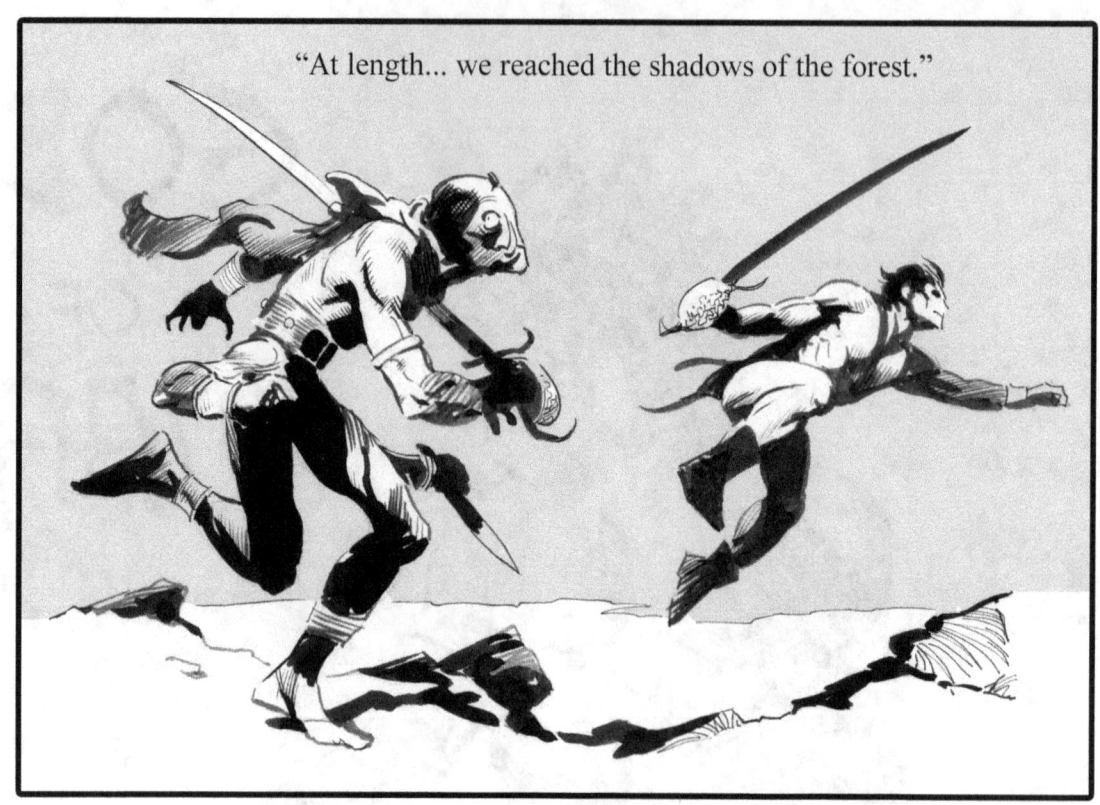

"At length... we reached the shadows of the forest."

"As it crept toward me it lashed its powerful tail against its yellow sides..."

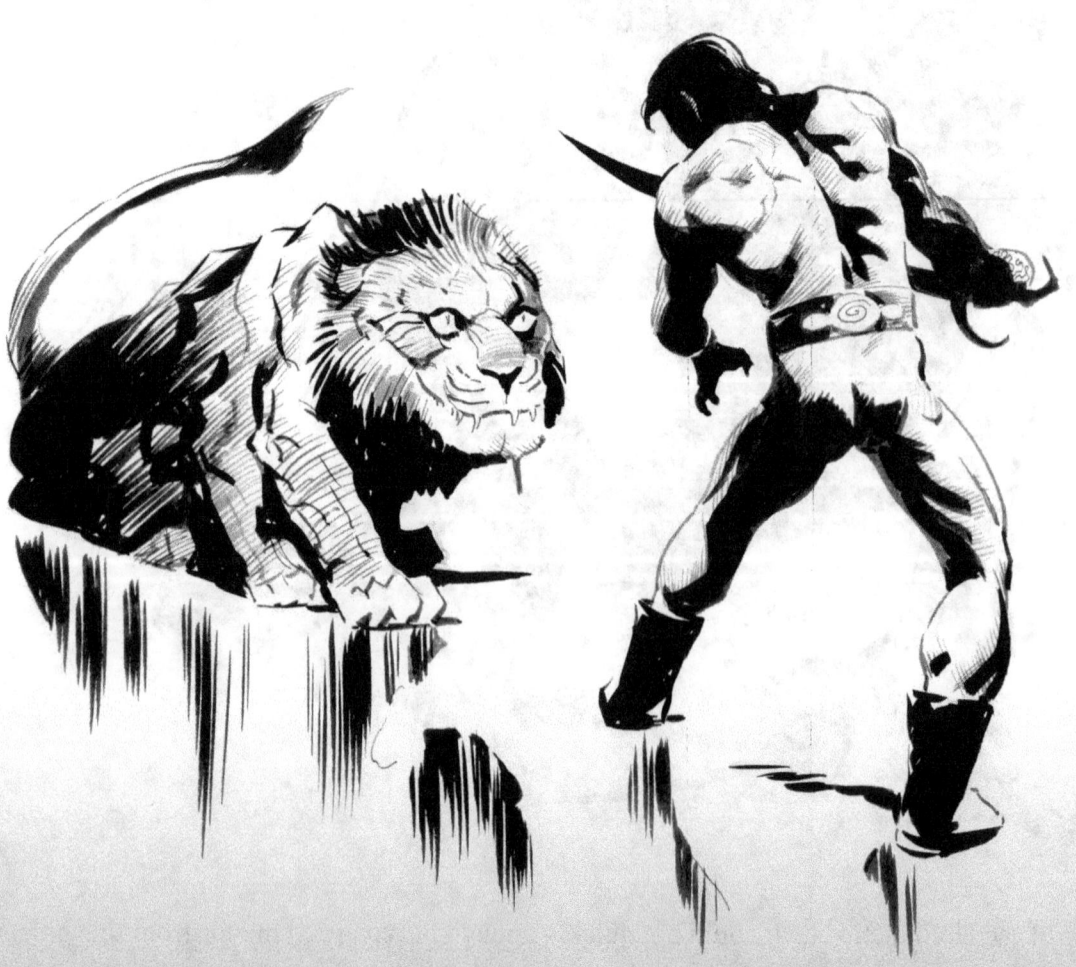

"It was into the eyes of such as these
and the terrible plant men that I gazed
above the shoulder of my foe..."

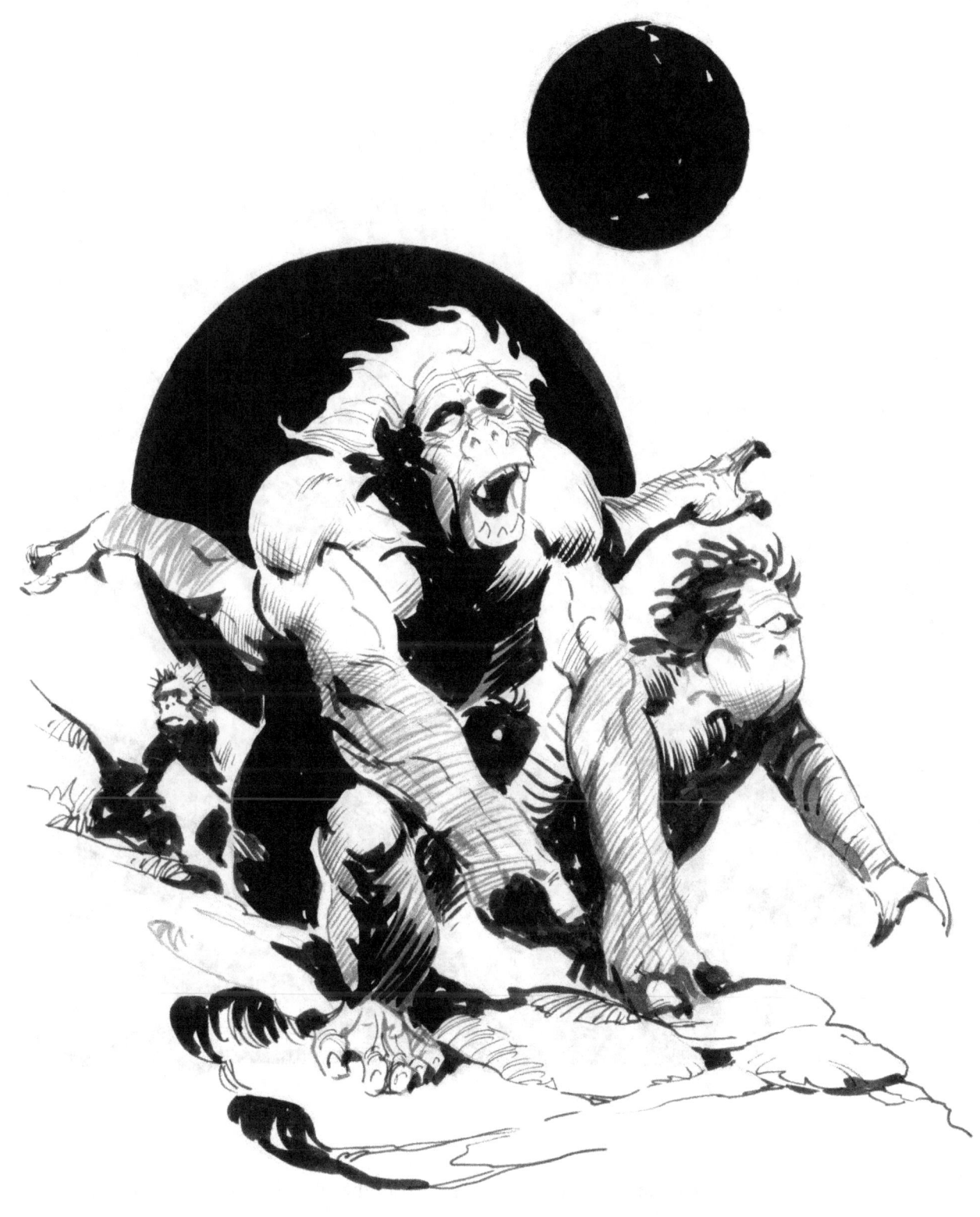

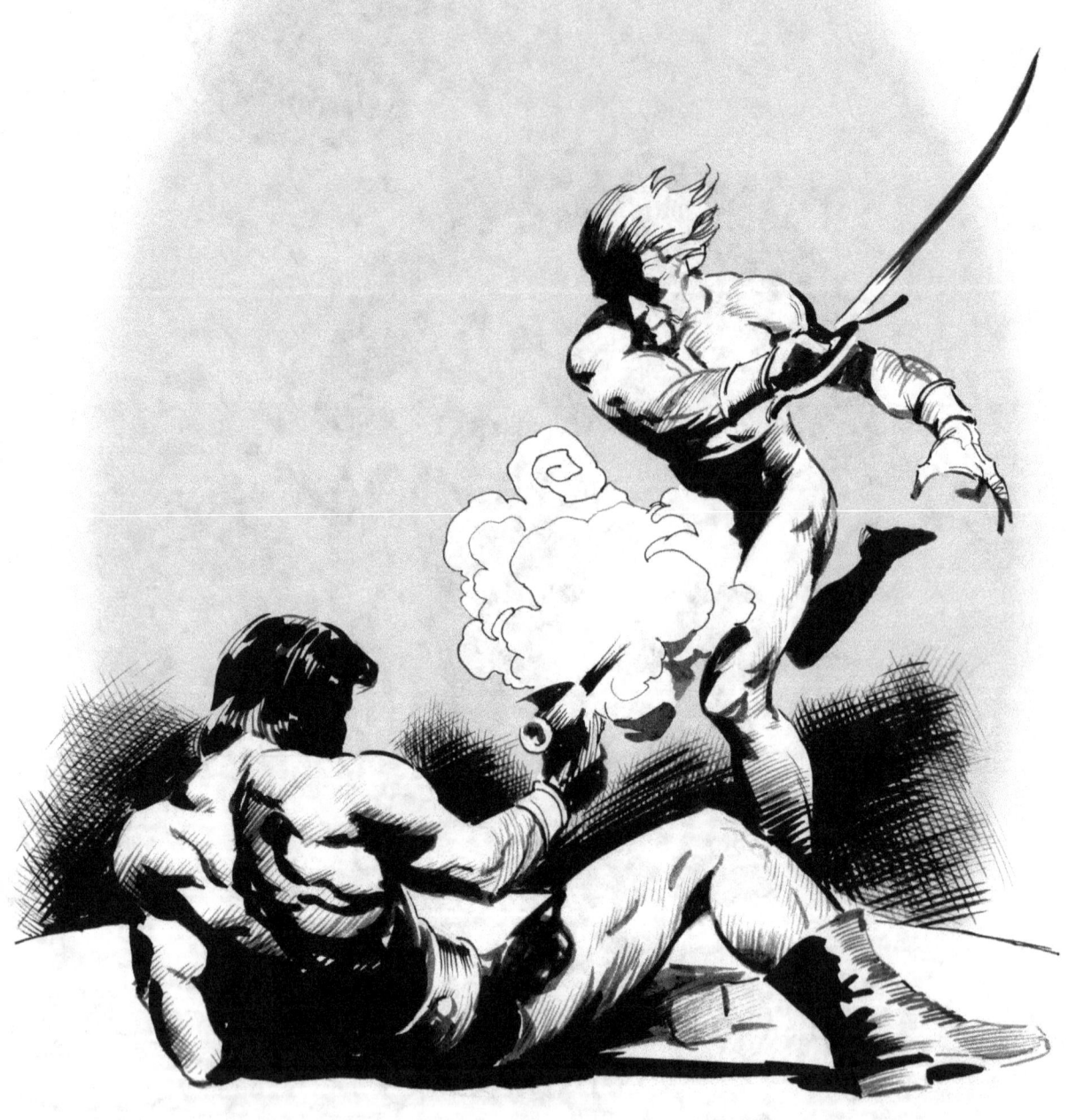

"And so he died, his thin lips curled in the snarl of his hateful laugh,
and a bullet from the revolver of his dead companion bursting in his heart."

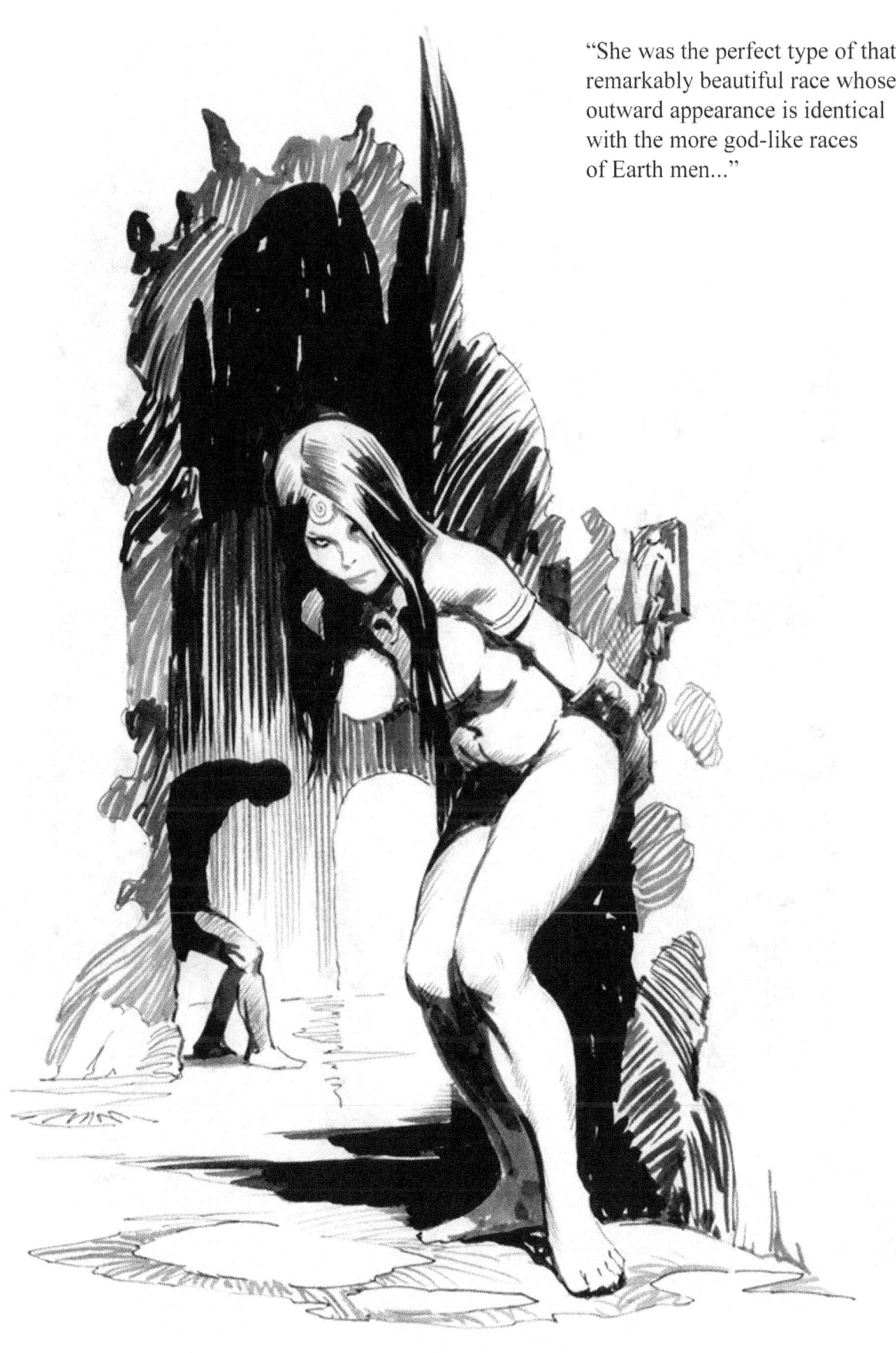

"She was the perfect type of that remarkably beautiful race whose outward appearance is identical with the more god-like races of Earth men..."

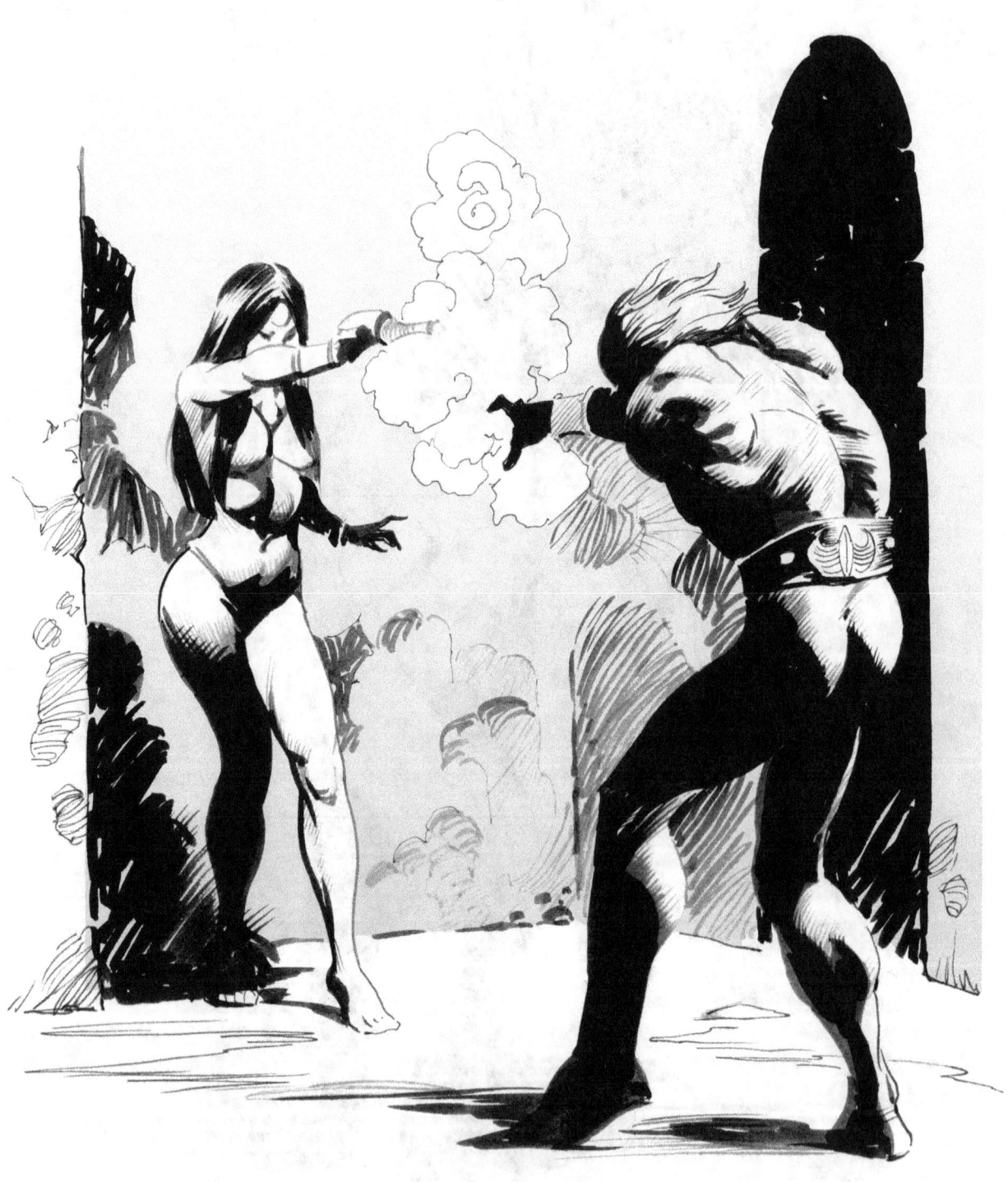

"For answer the girl raised her revolver and fired point-blank at him."

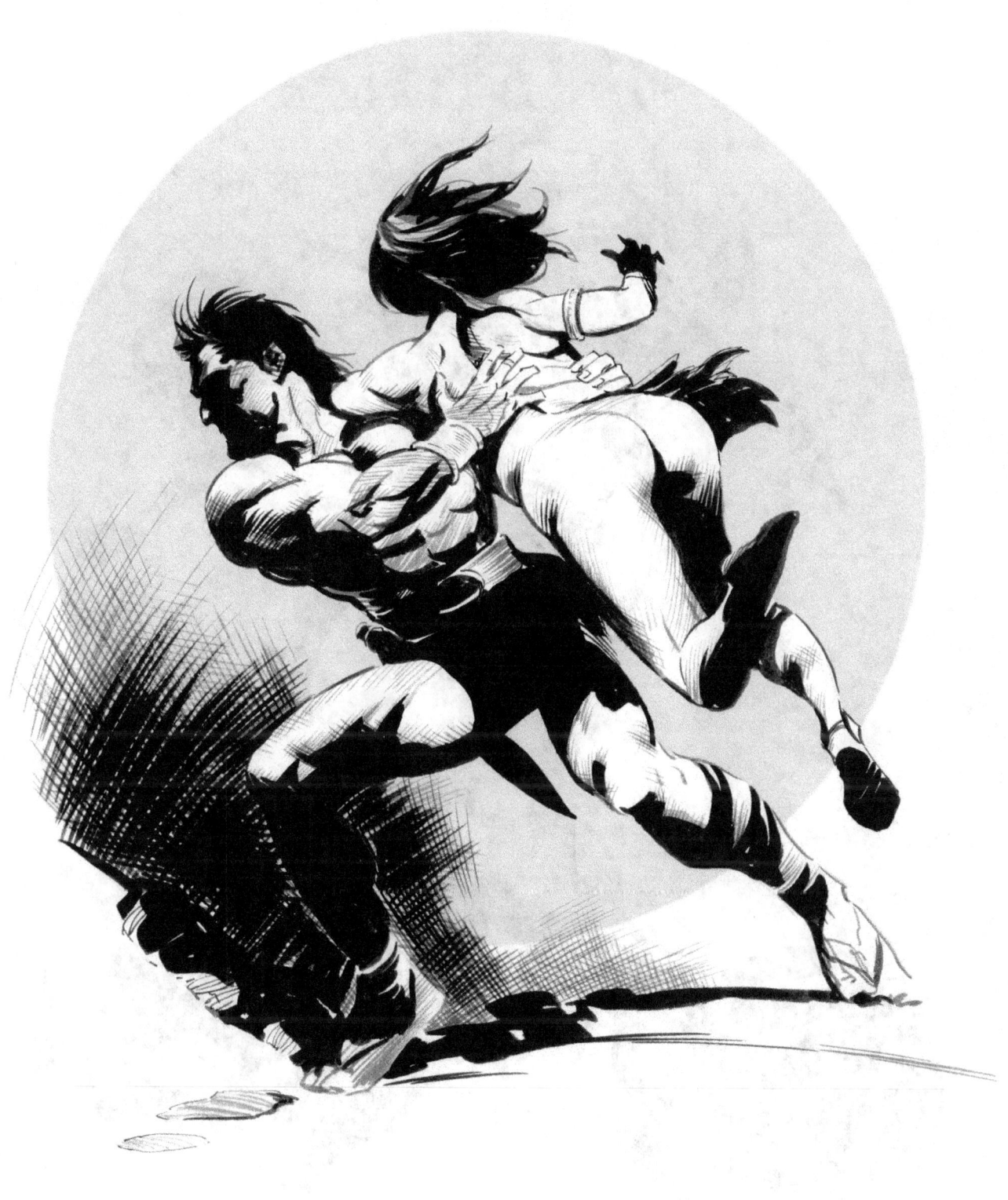

"Where they visited they wrought the most horrible atrocities, and when
they left carried away with them firearms and ammunition, and young girls as prisoners."

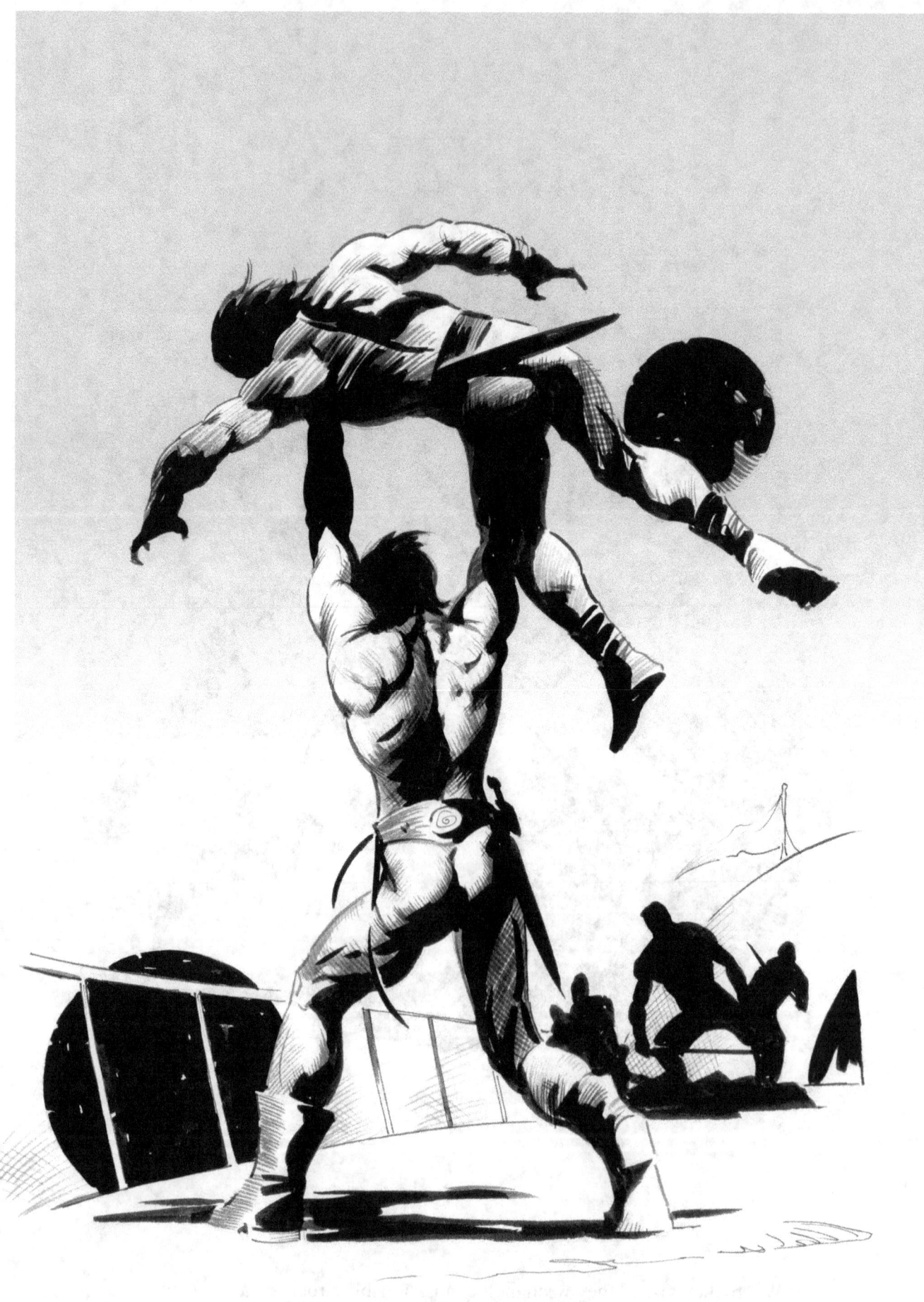

"...I released my hold upon him and in an instant he was swallowed by the black shadows far below."

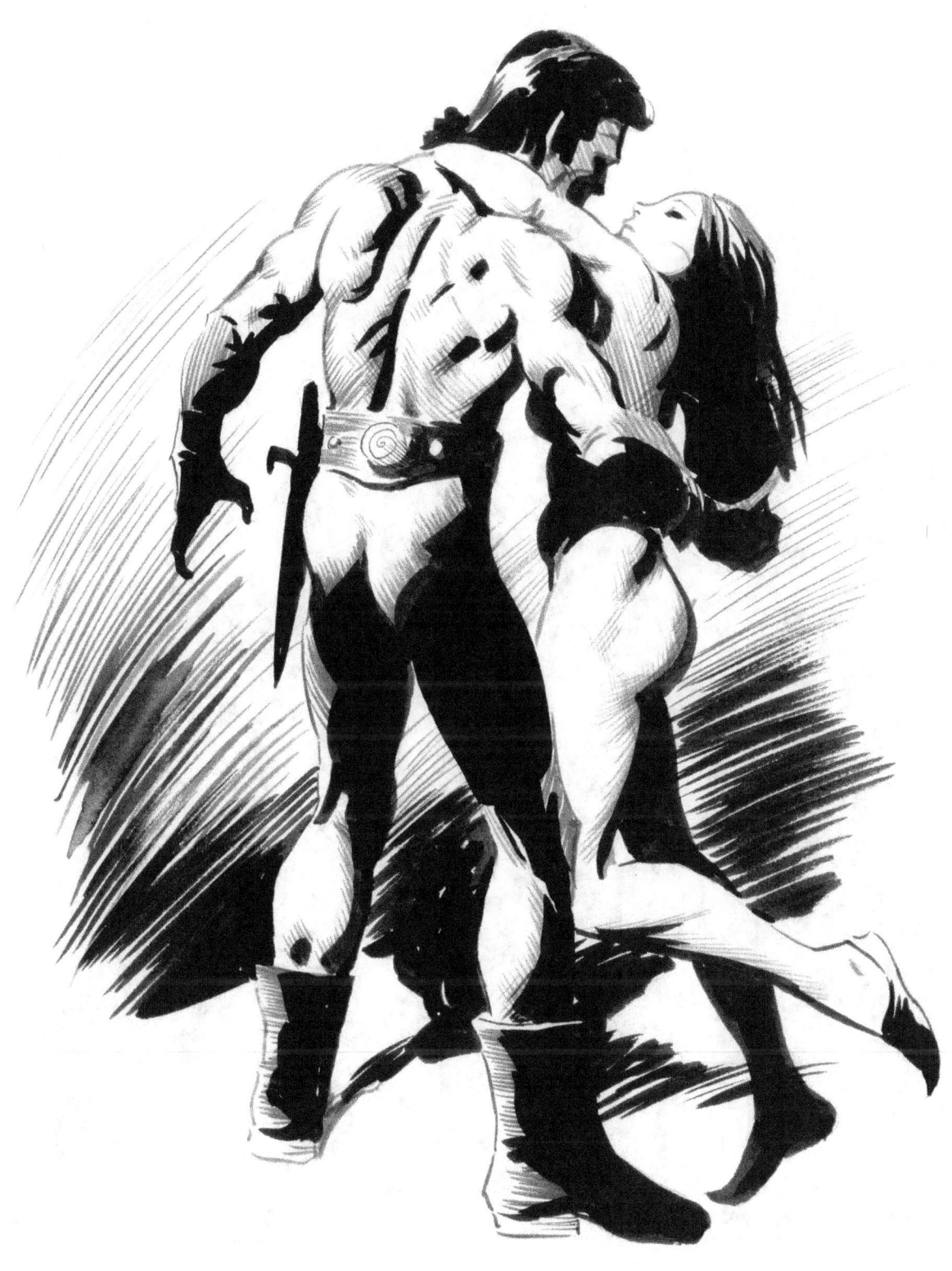

"...she threw both her arms about my neck and dragged my face down to hers."

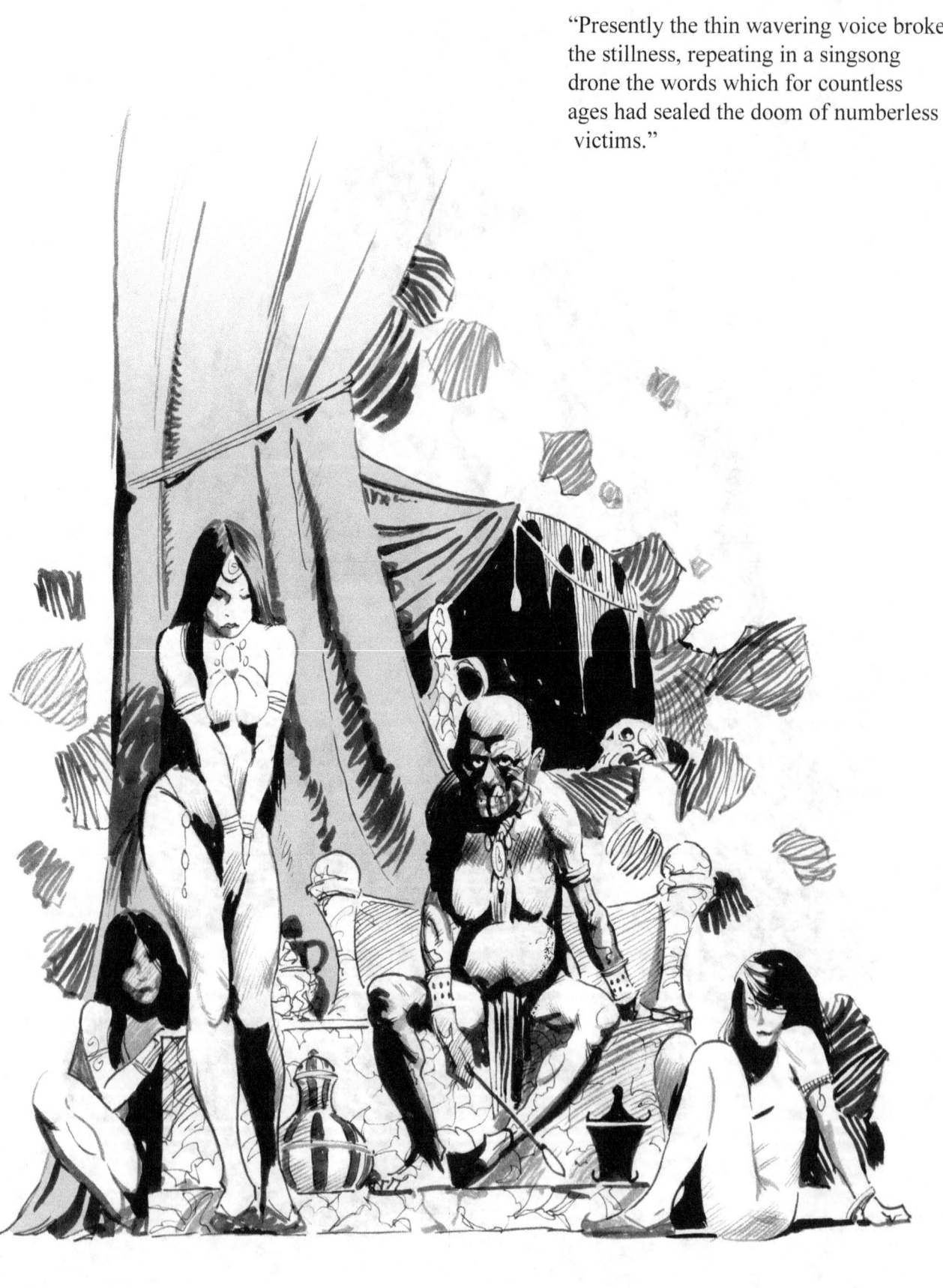

"Presently the thin wavering voice broke
the stillness, repeating in a singsong
drone the words which for countless
ages had sealed the doom of numberless
 victims."

"I scrambled up the iron grating of the window until I could catch a good footing on the sill with one foot..."

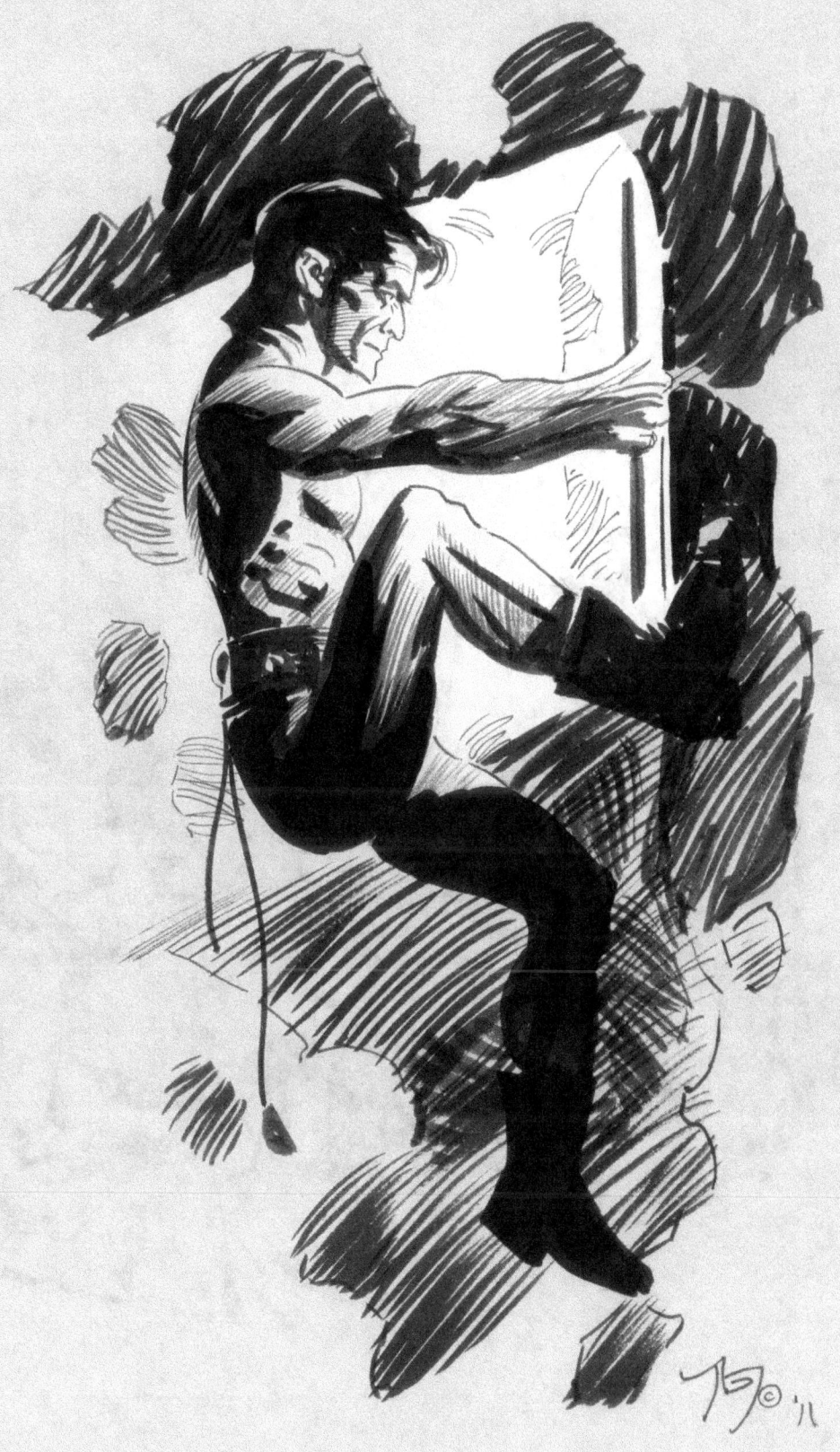

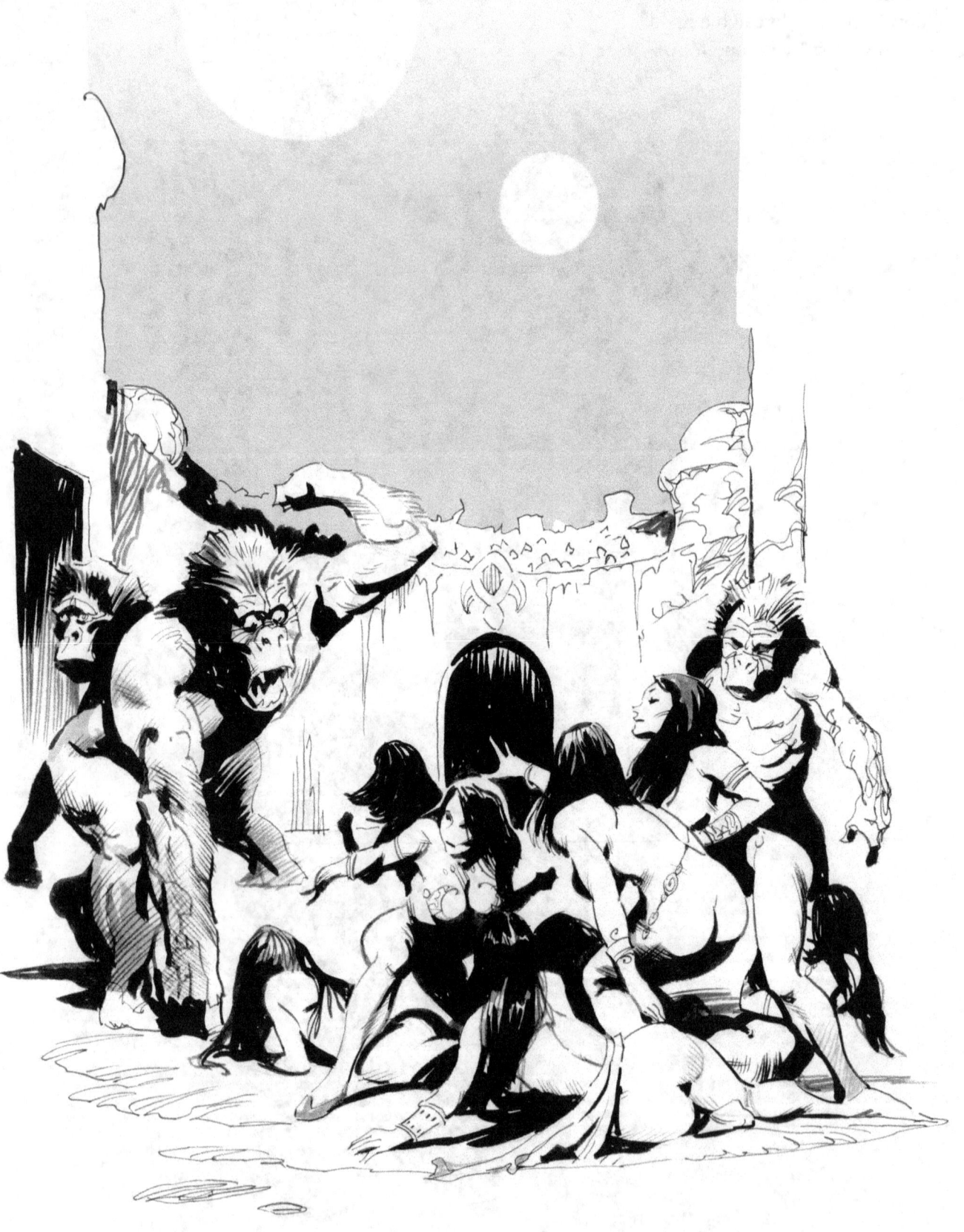

"The first event of the day was the Tribute to Issus.
It marked the end of those poor unfortunates who
had looked upon the divine glory of the goddess
a full year before."

"...ere he fell I snatched the girl from his back and
swung her to a place upon my own thoat."

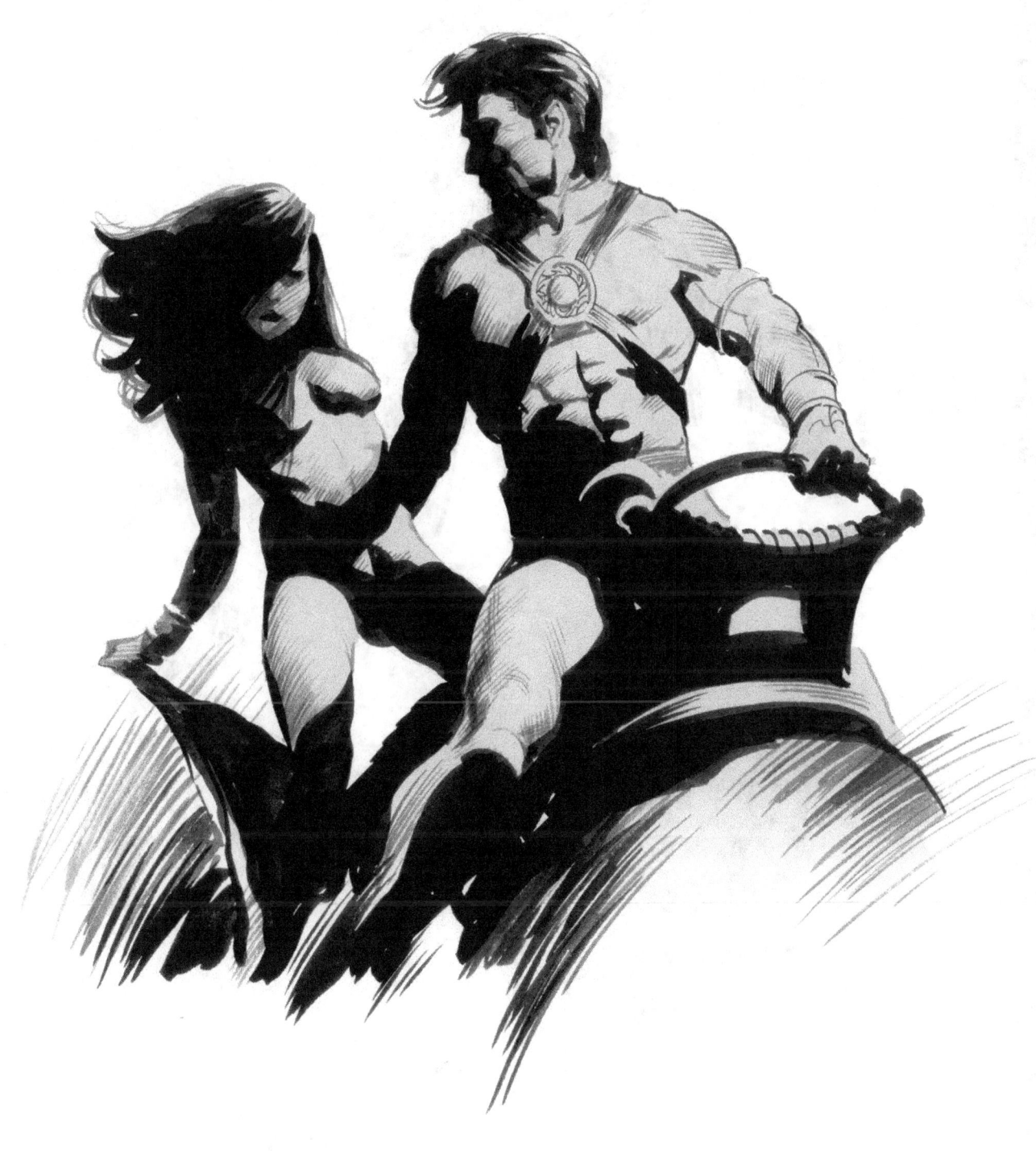

"The cruiser, already tilted at a perilous angle, was carried completely
over backward by the impact of my smaller vessel."

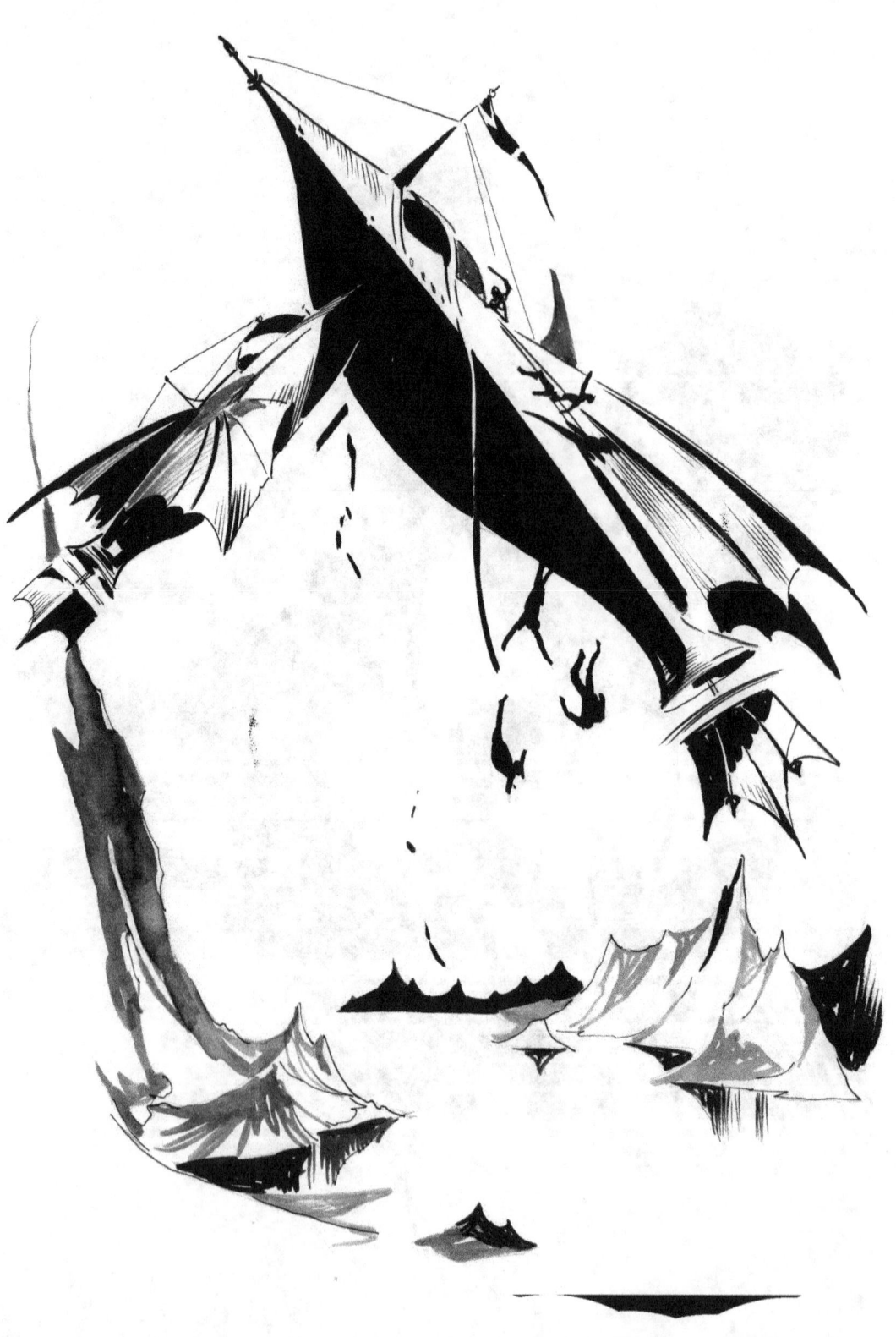

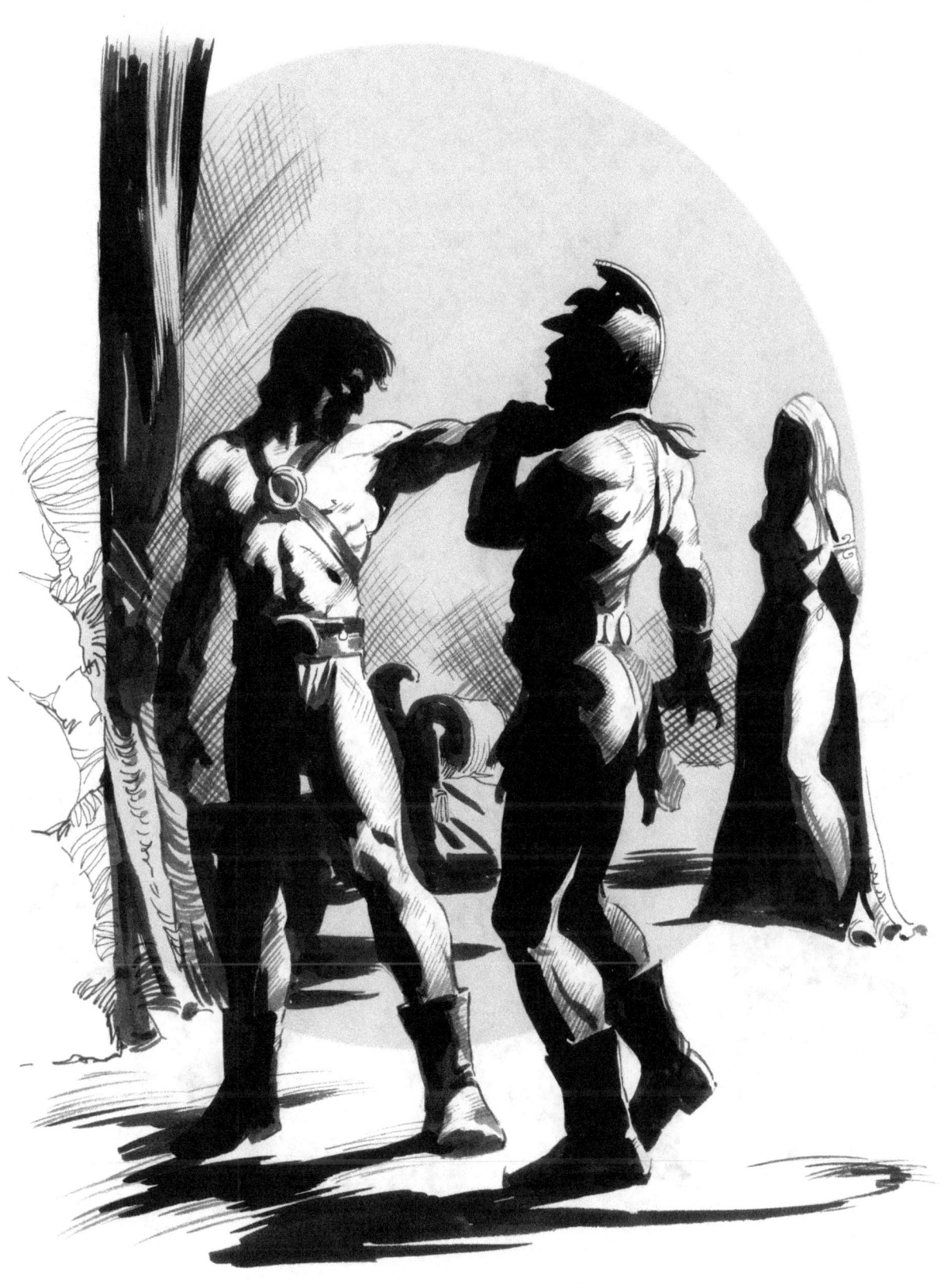

"Before a hand could be raised to stop me, I was at his side and one hand grasped his throat."

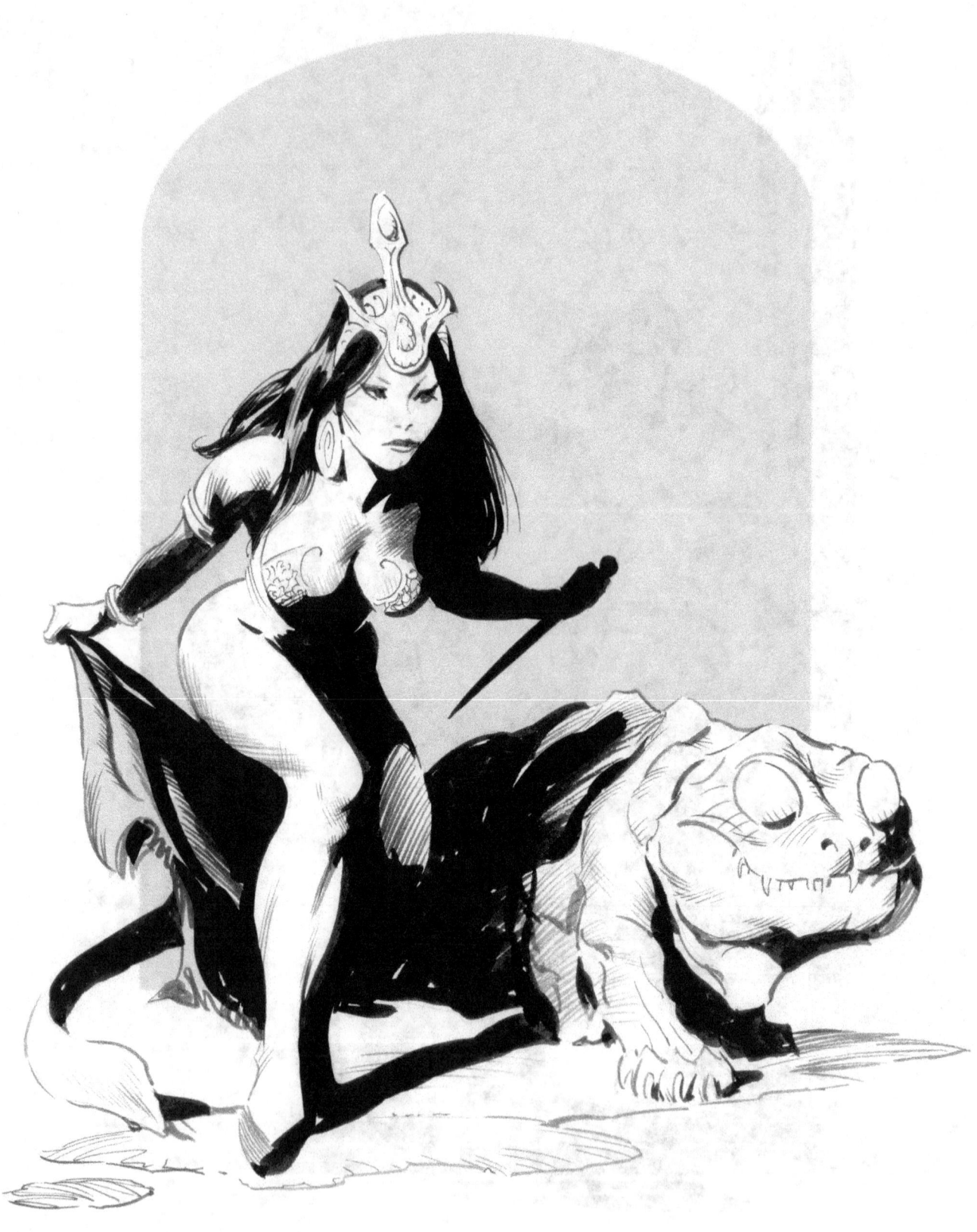

"With her was faithful Woola the hound,
but none other. When we overtook her she feigned anger,
and ordered us back to the palace..."

"I was alone with my gruesome companions--with the bones of dead men whose fate was likely but the index of my own."

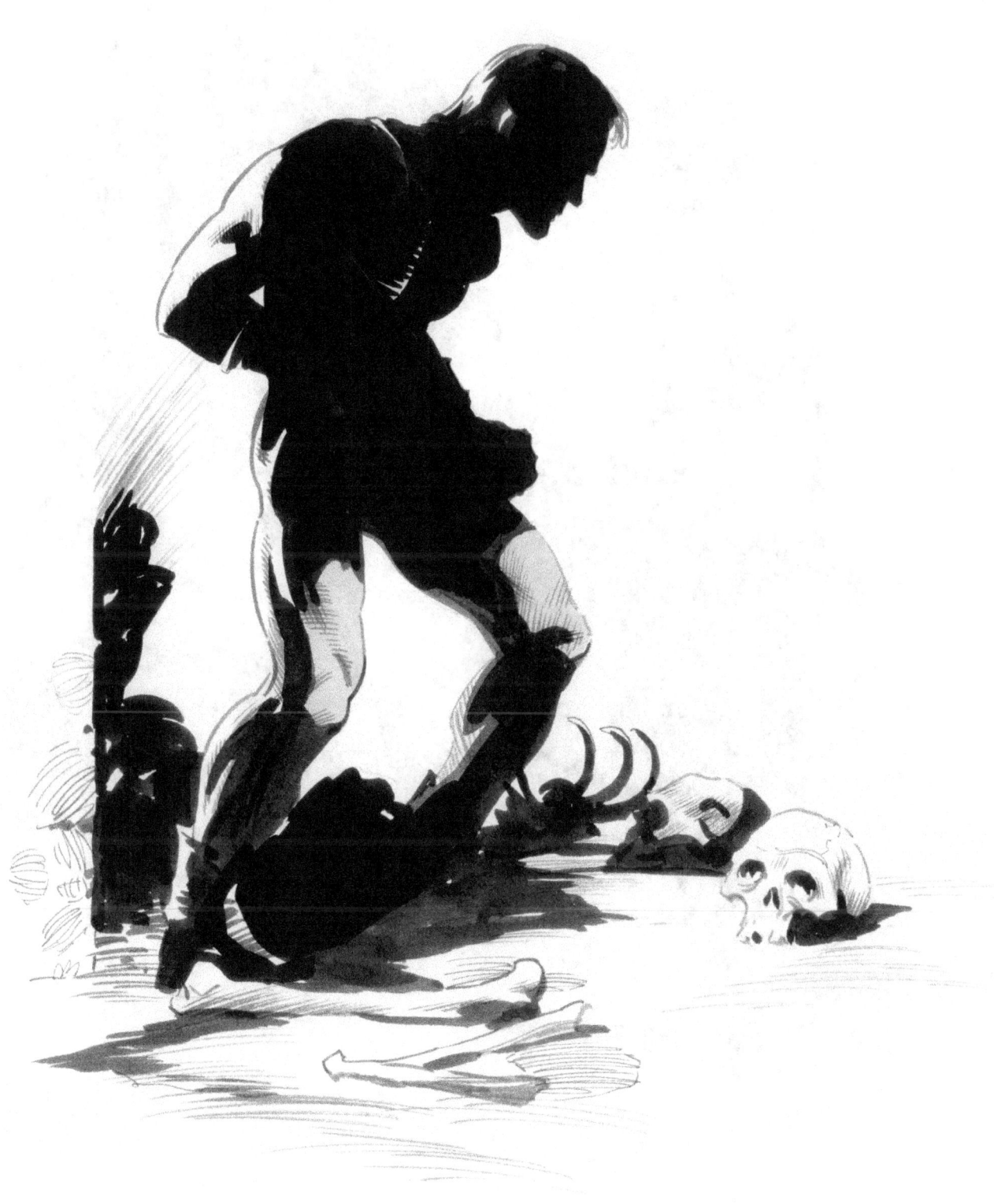

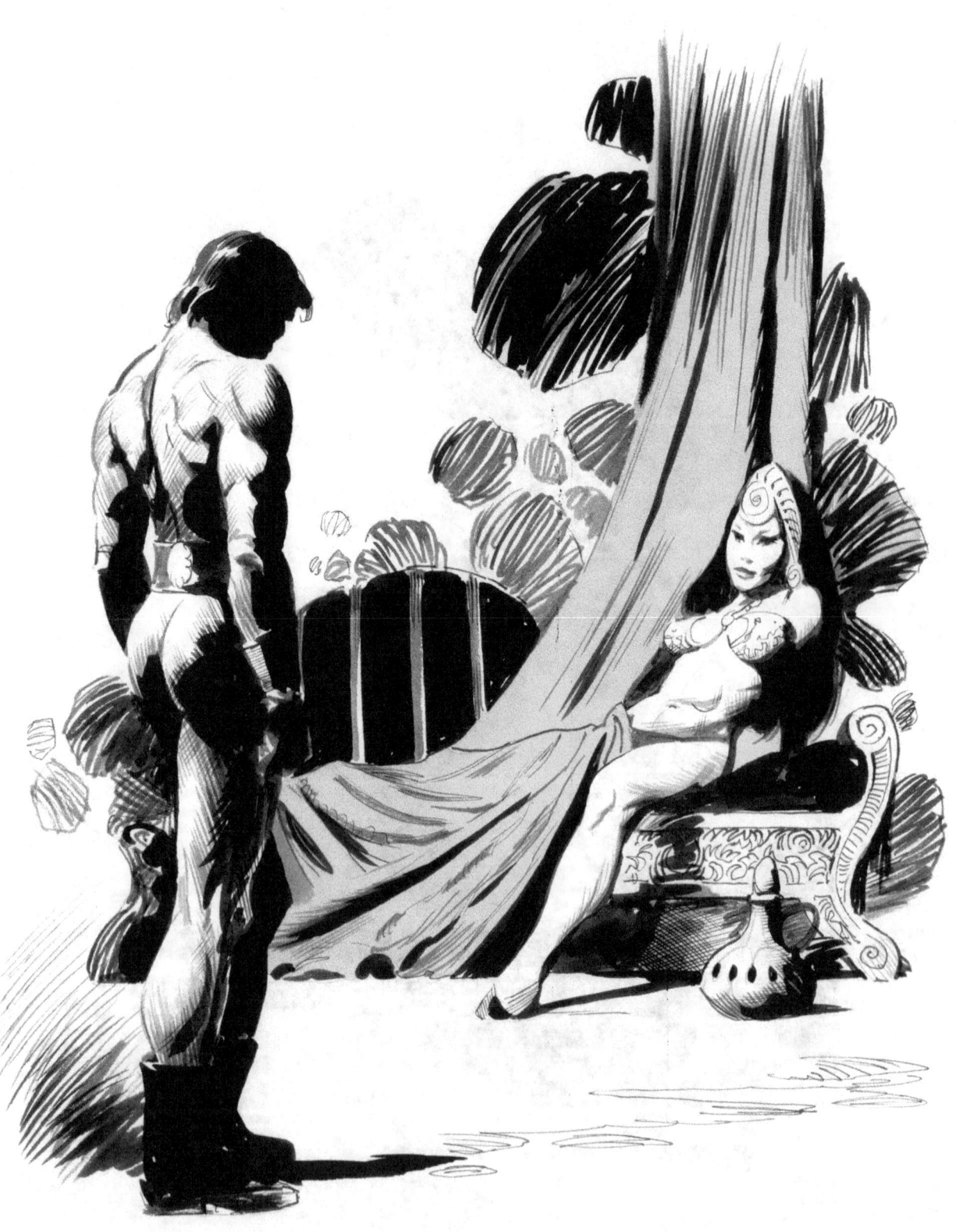

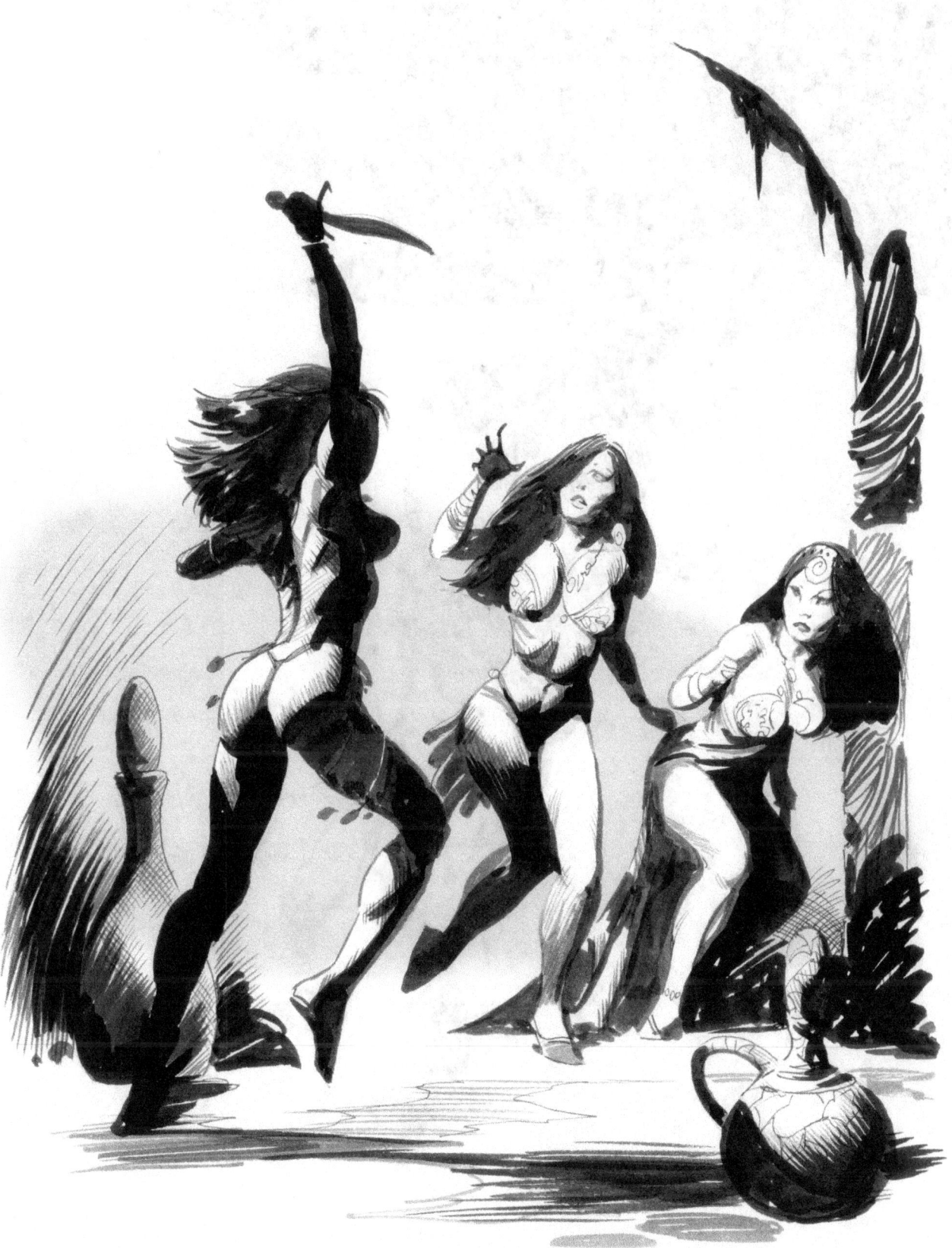

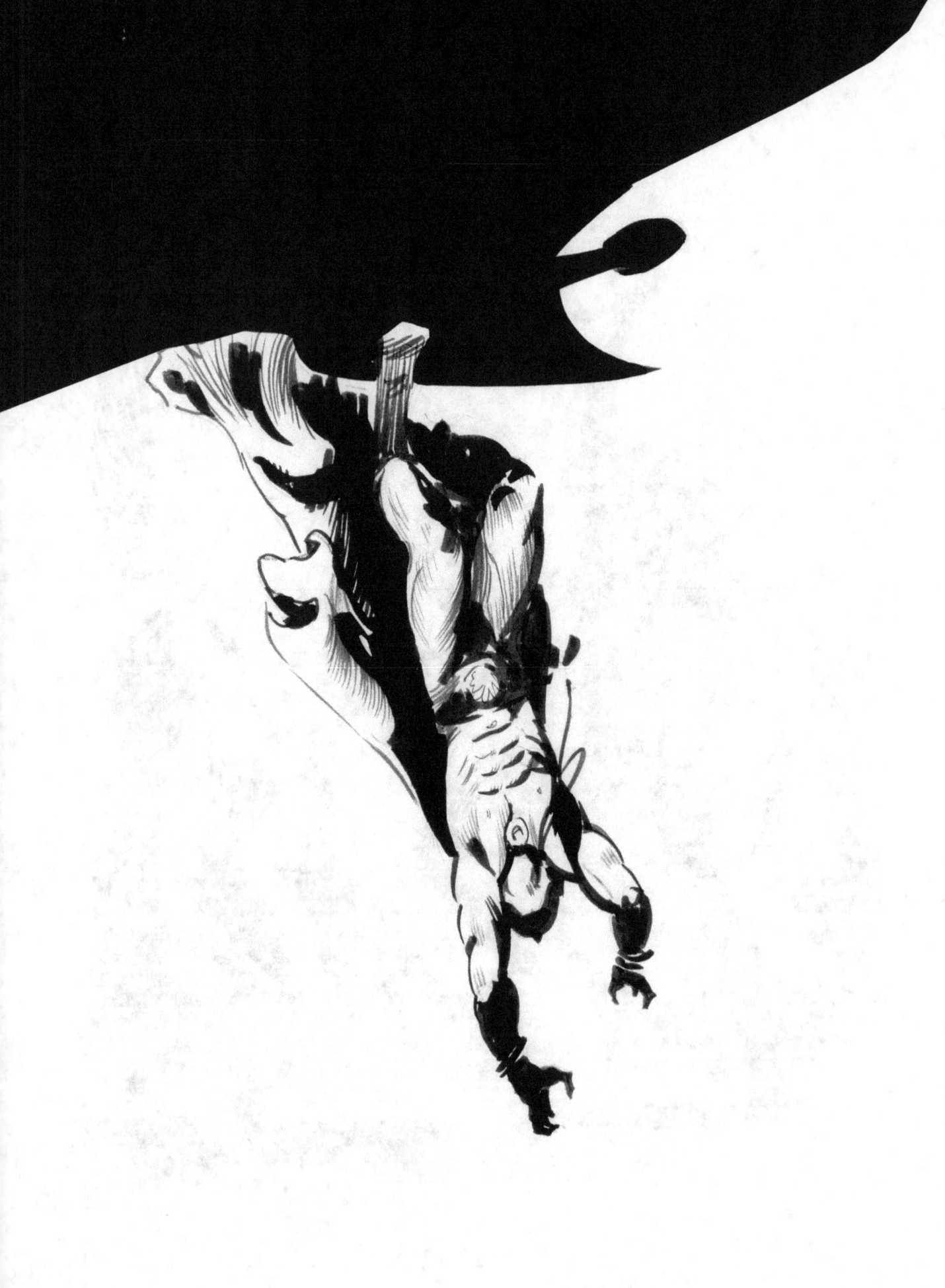

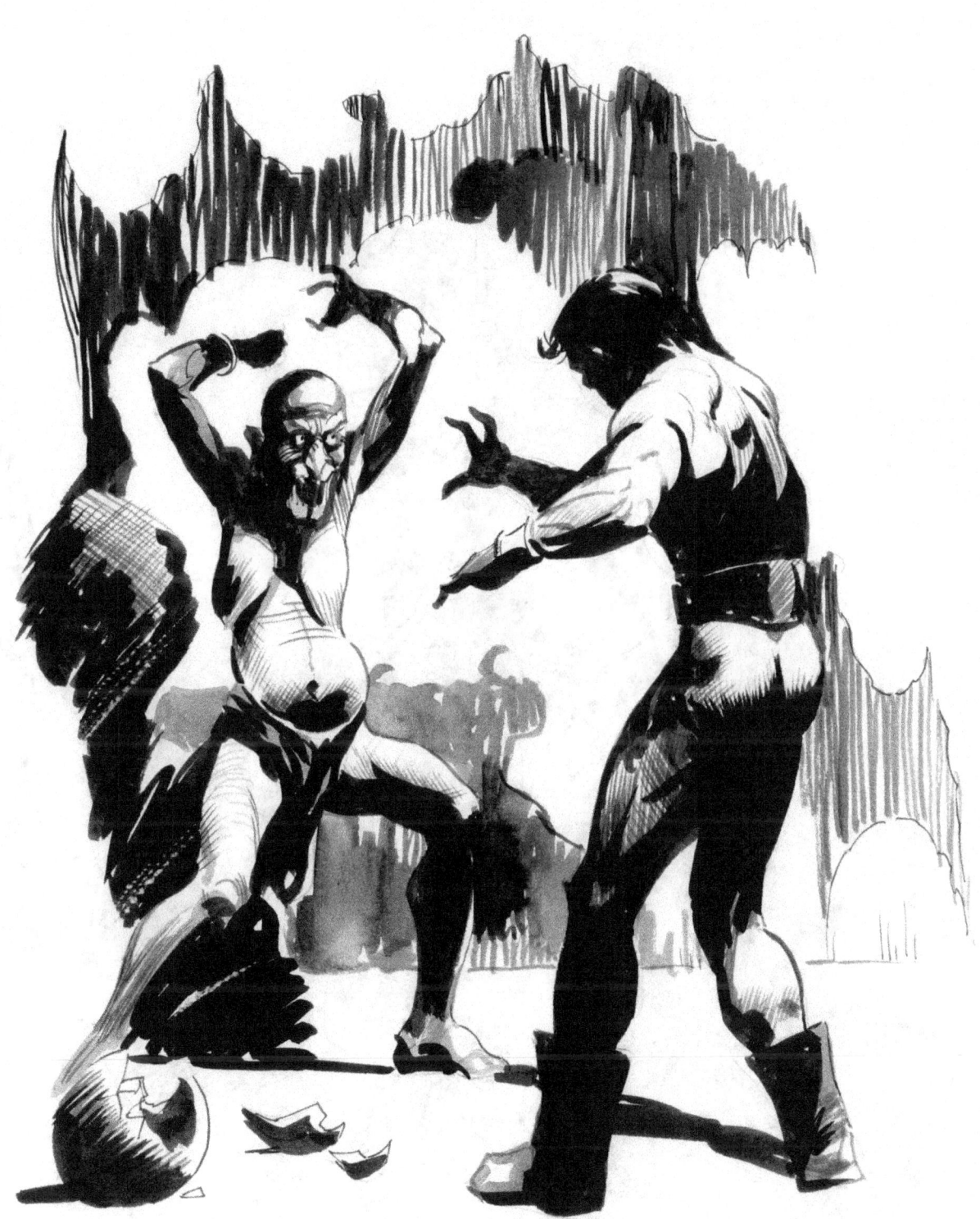

WARLORD
OF
MARS

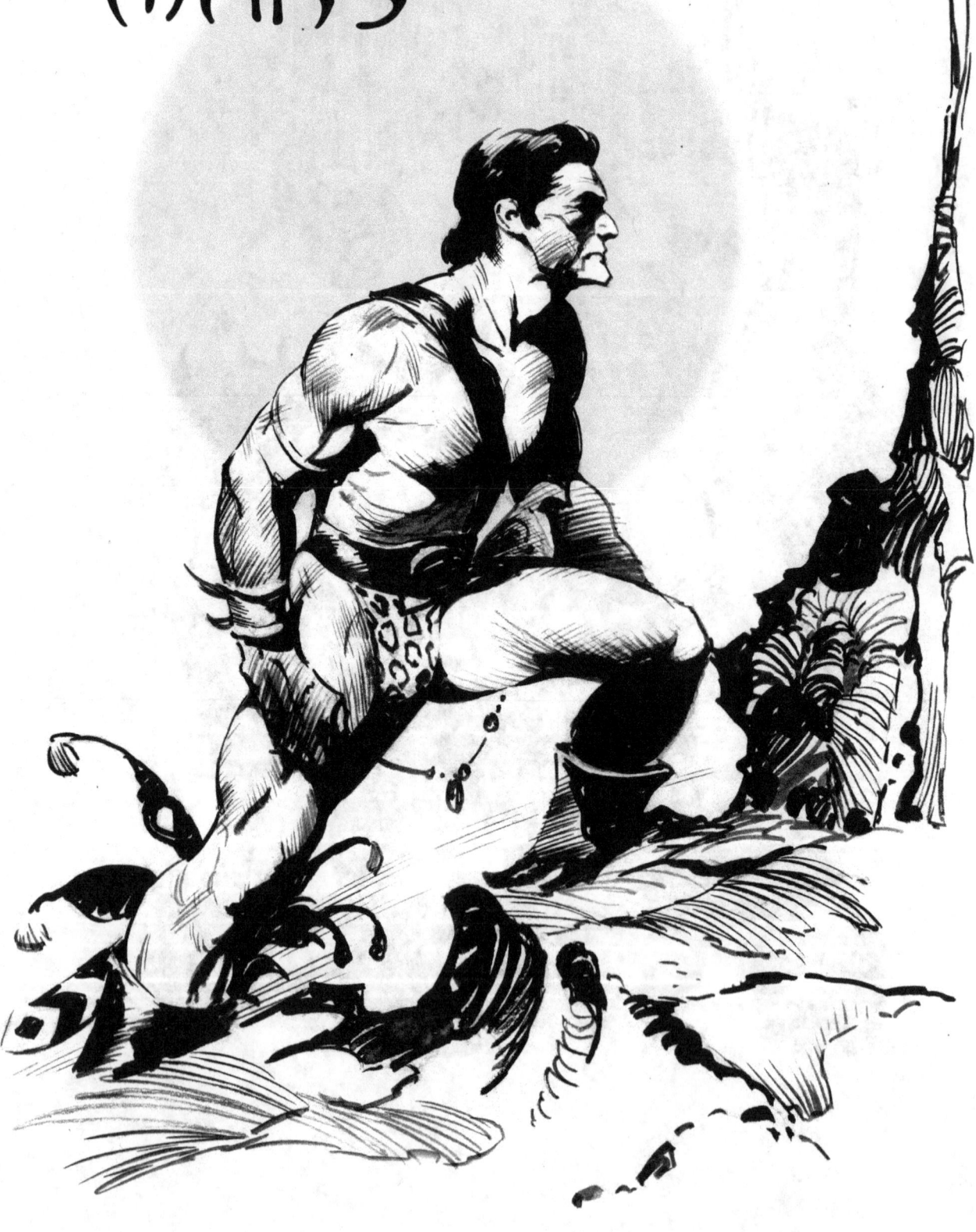

"So it was that I remained hidden until after Thurid had disappeared over the edge of the steep bank beside the sea a quarter of a mile away. Then, with Woola following, I hastened across the open after the black dator."

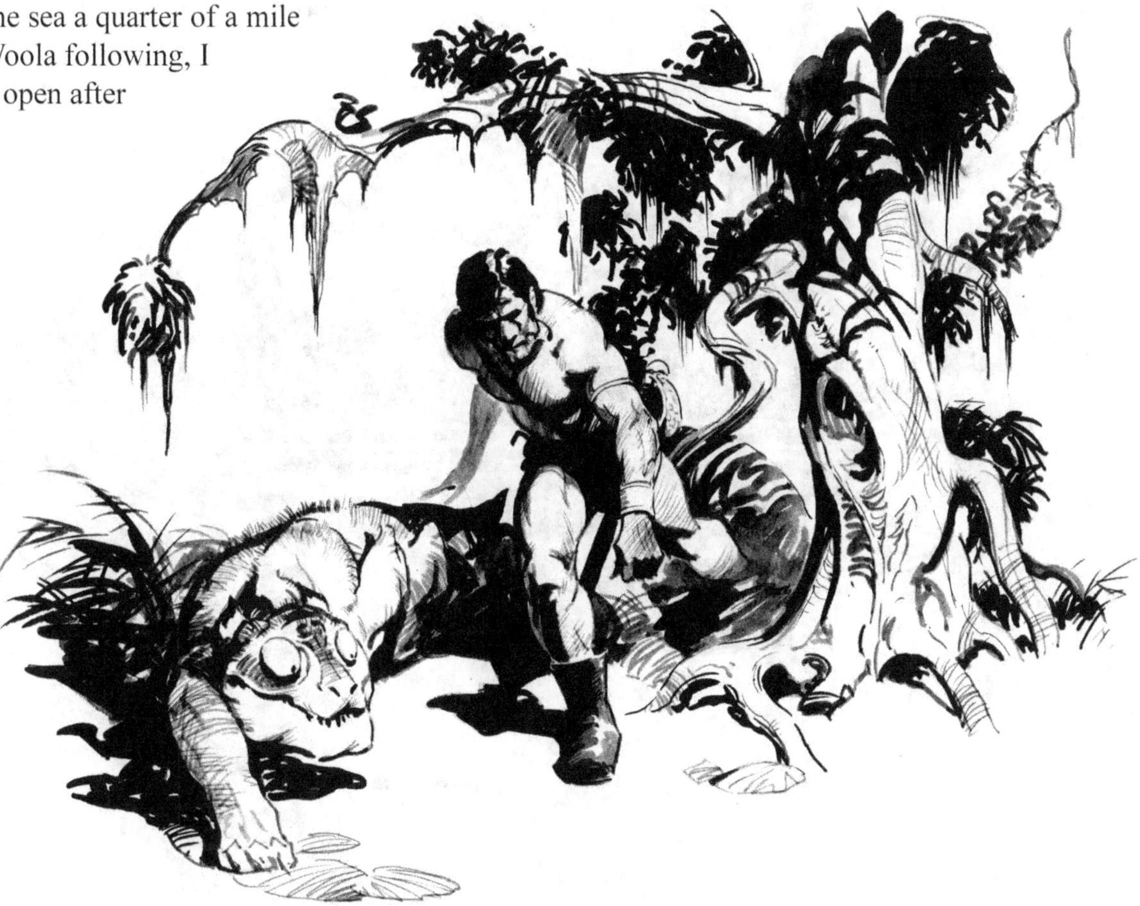

"In the awful stench of these frightful charnel isles haggard maniacs screamed and gibbered and fought among the torn remnants of their grisly feasts..."

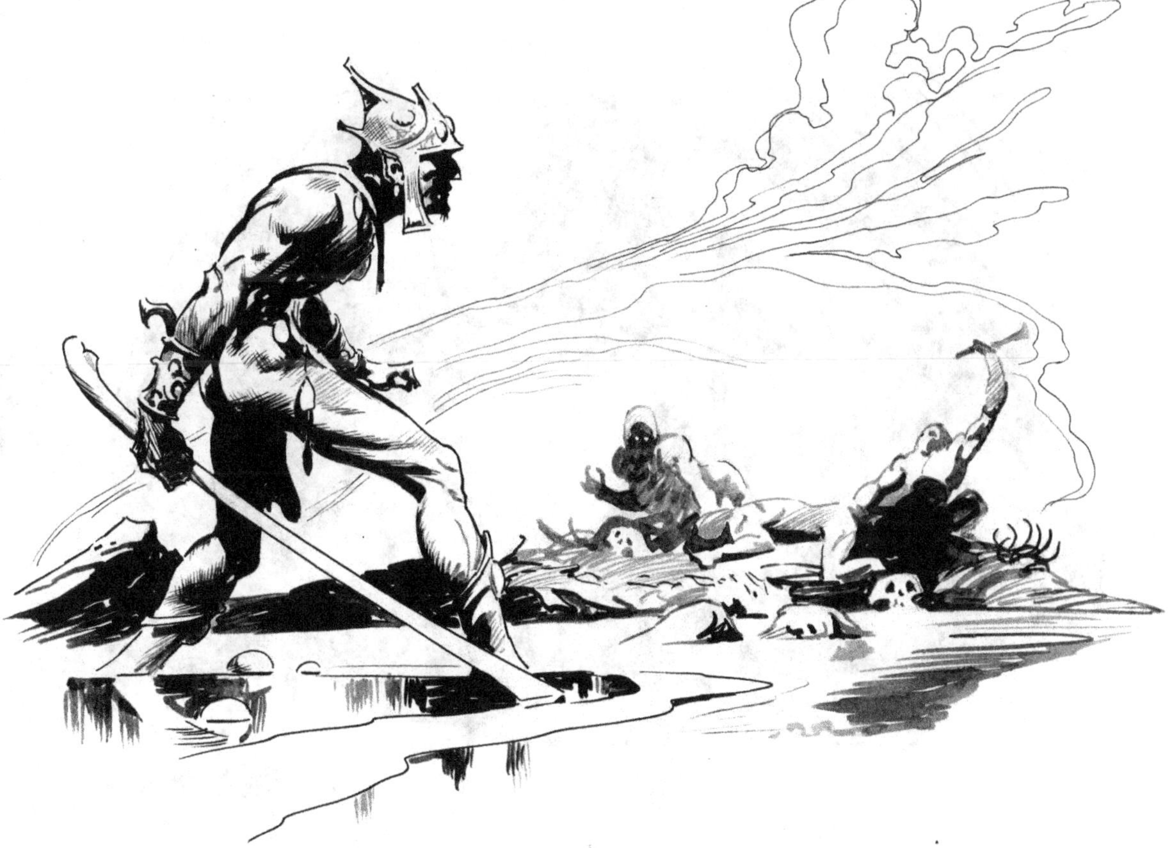

"I noticed that a strong current seemed to flow directly toward the center of the river..."

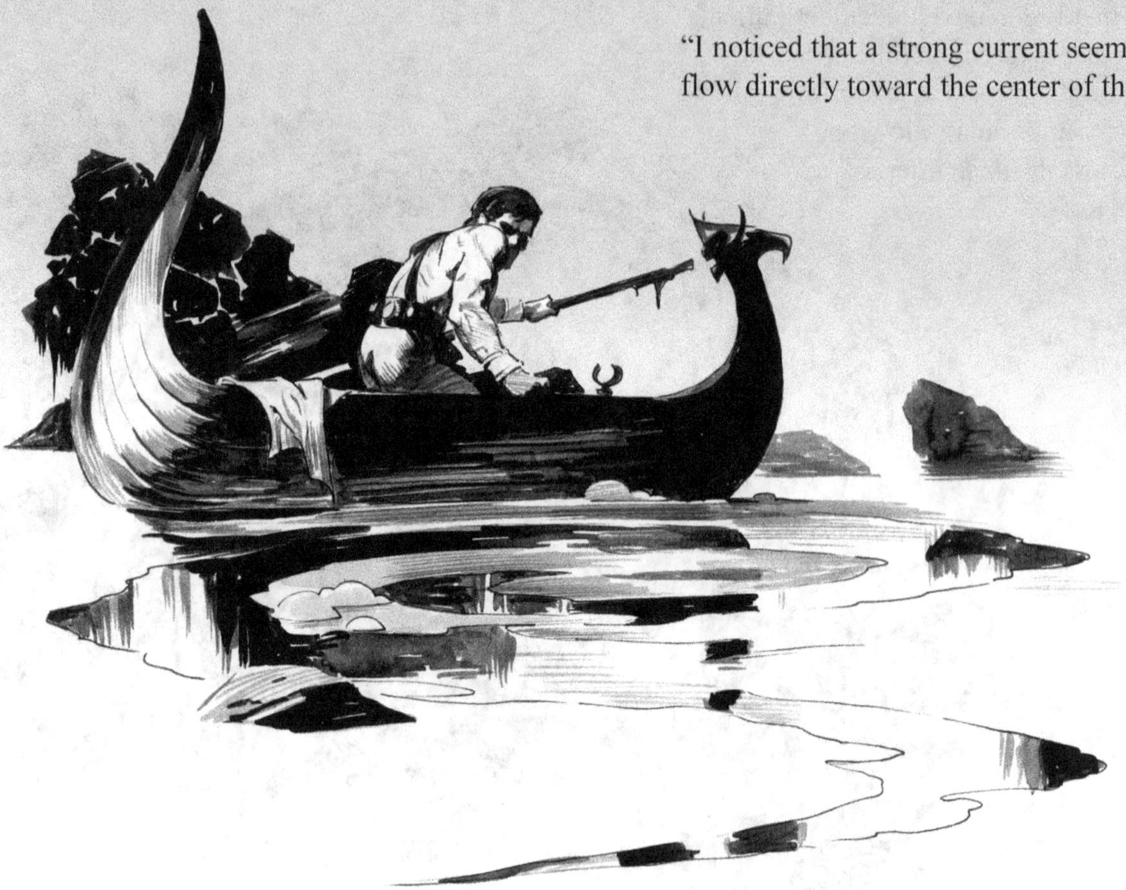

"The men were in earnest conversation, and from their tones it was apparent that they were entirely unaware that they had listeners."

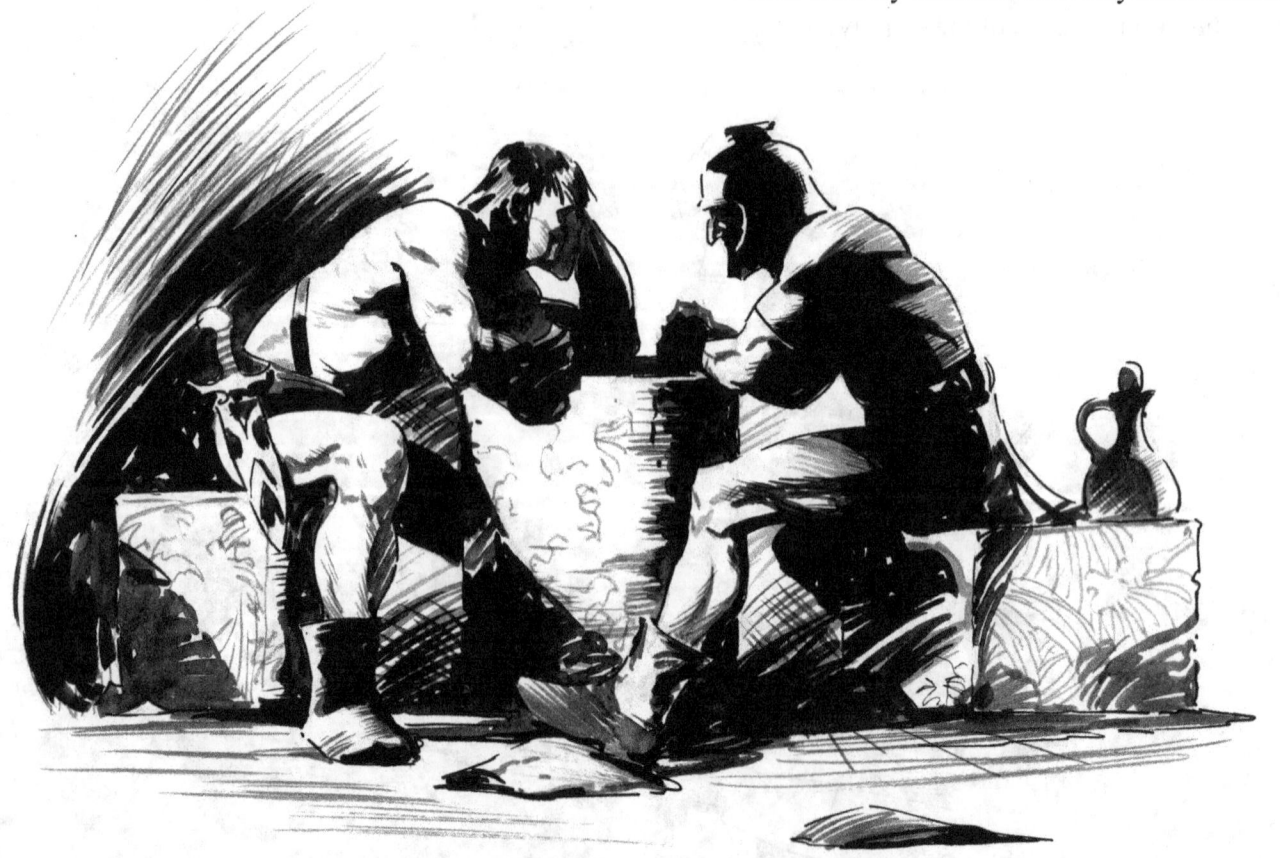

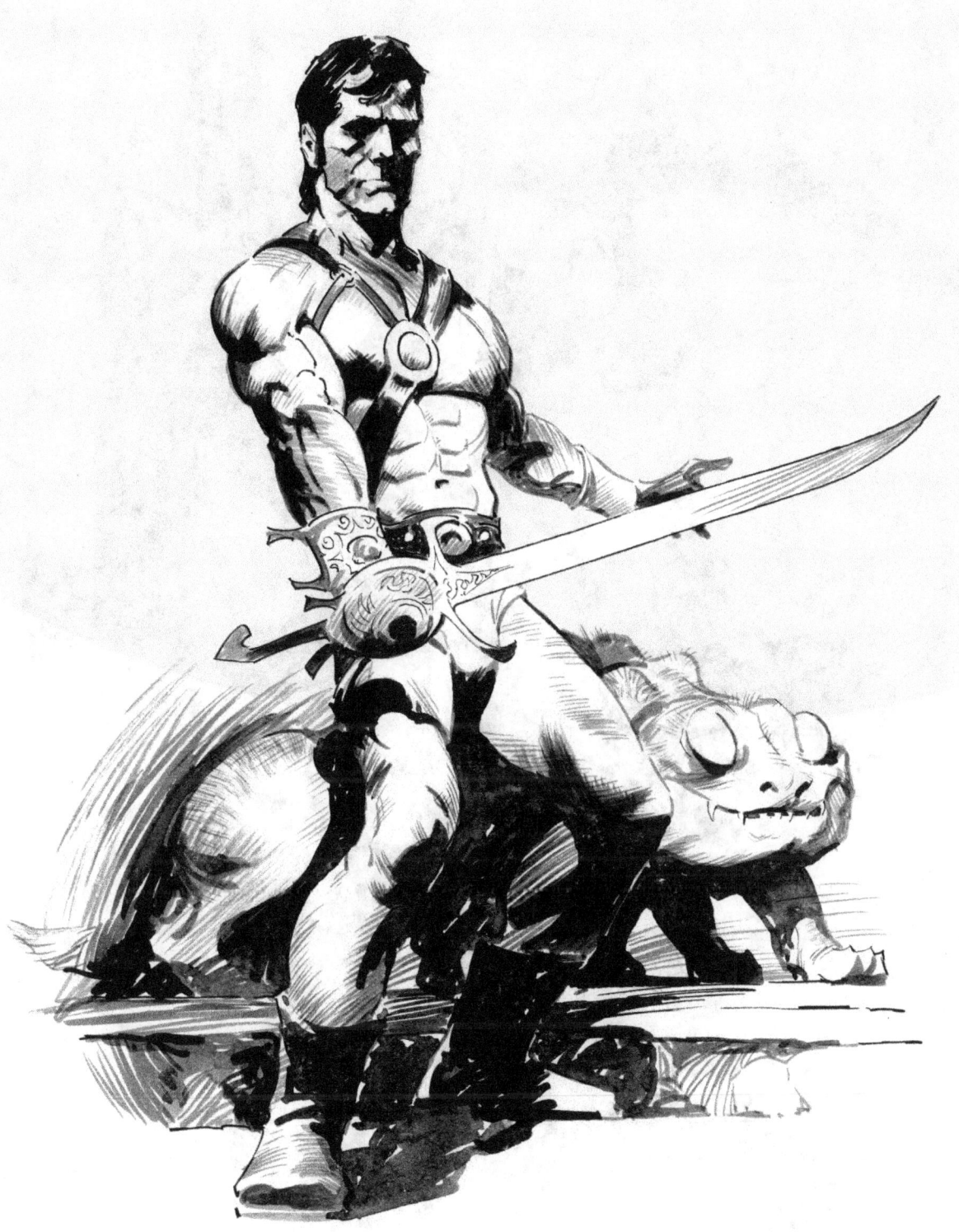

"Signaling Woola to heel I stepped suddenly
into the room before the two men."

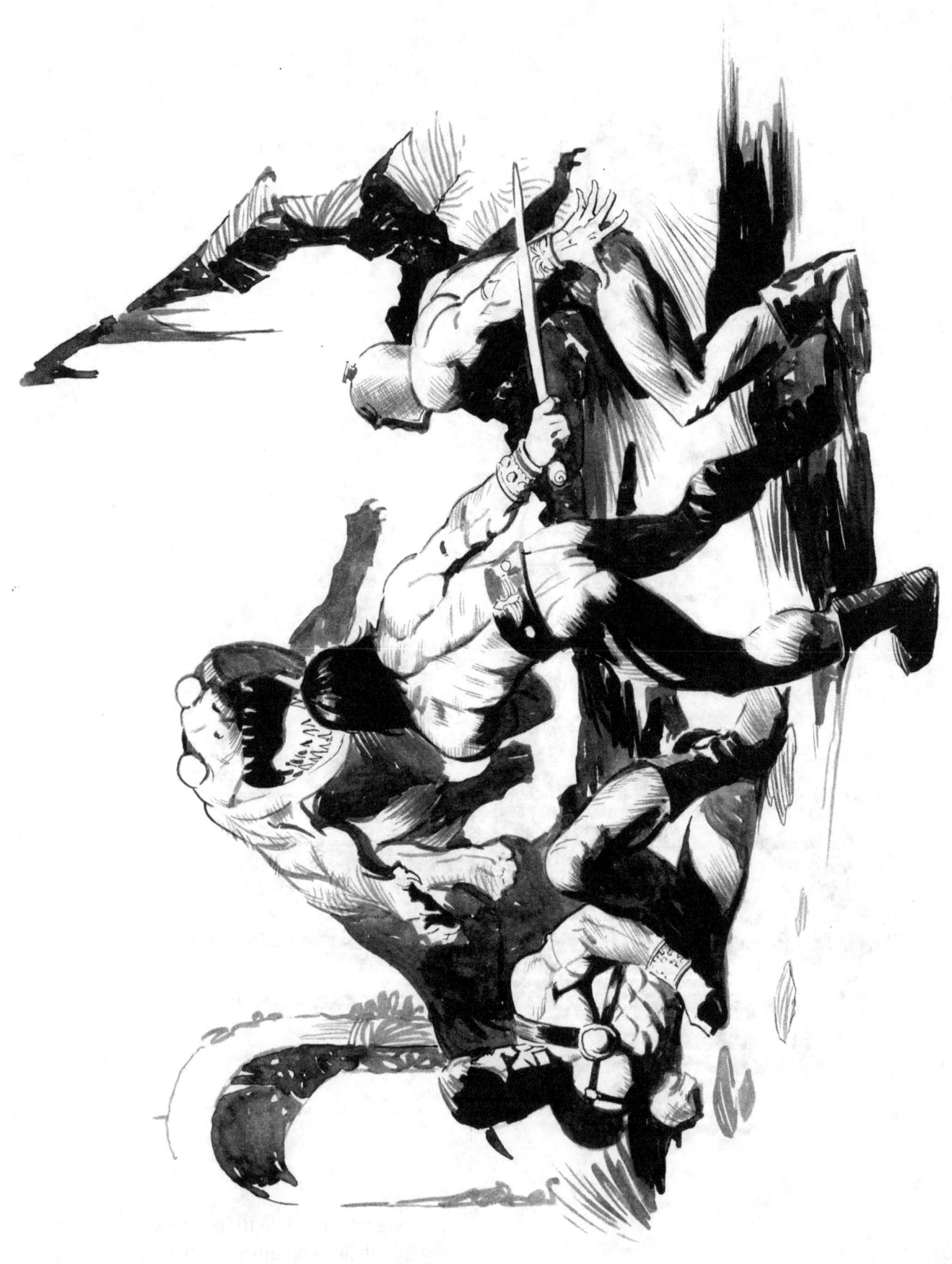

"While it lasted it was indeed as joyous a conflict as I ever had experienced."

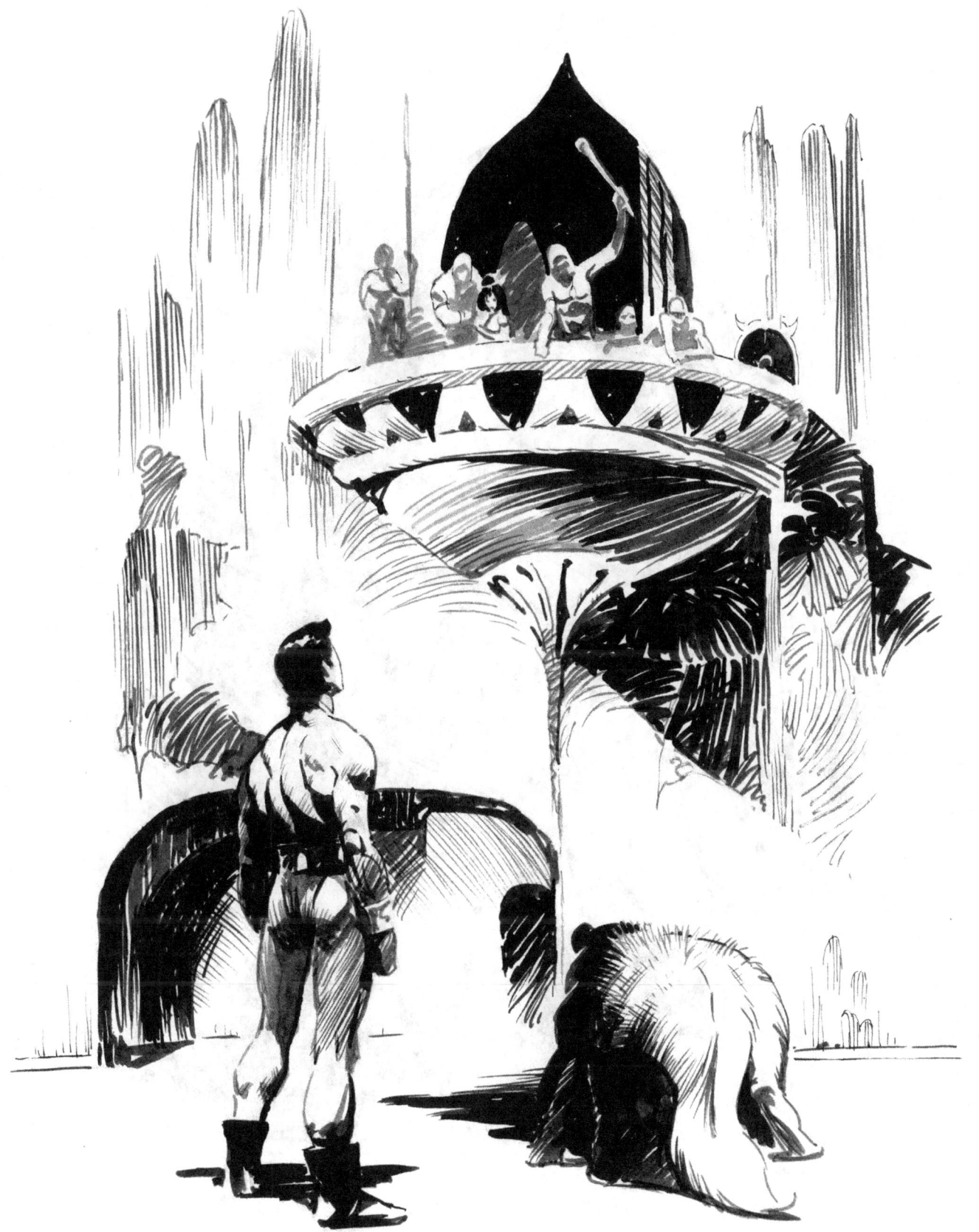

"...and there, indeed, was Matai Shang, and with him were Thurid and Phaidor, Thuvia, and Dejah Thoris--the last two heavily ironed."

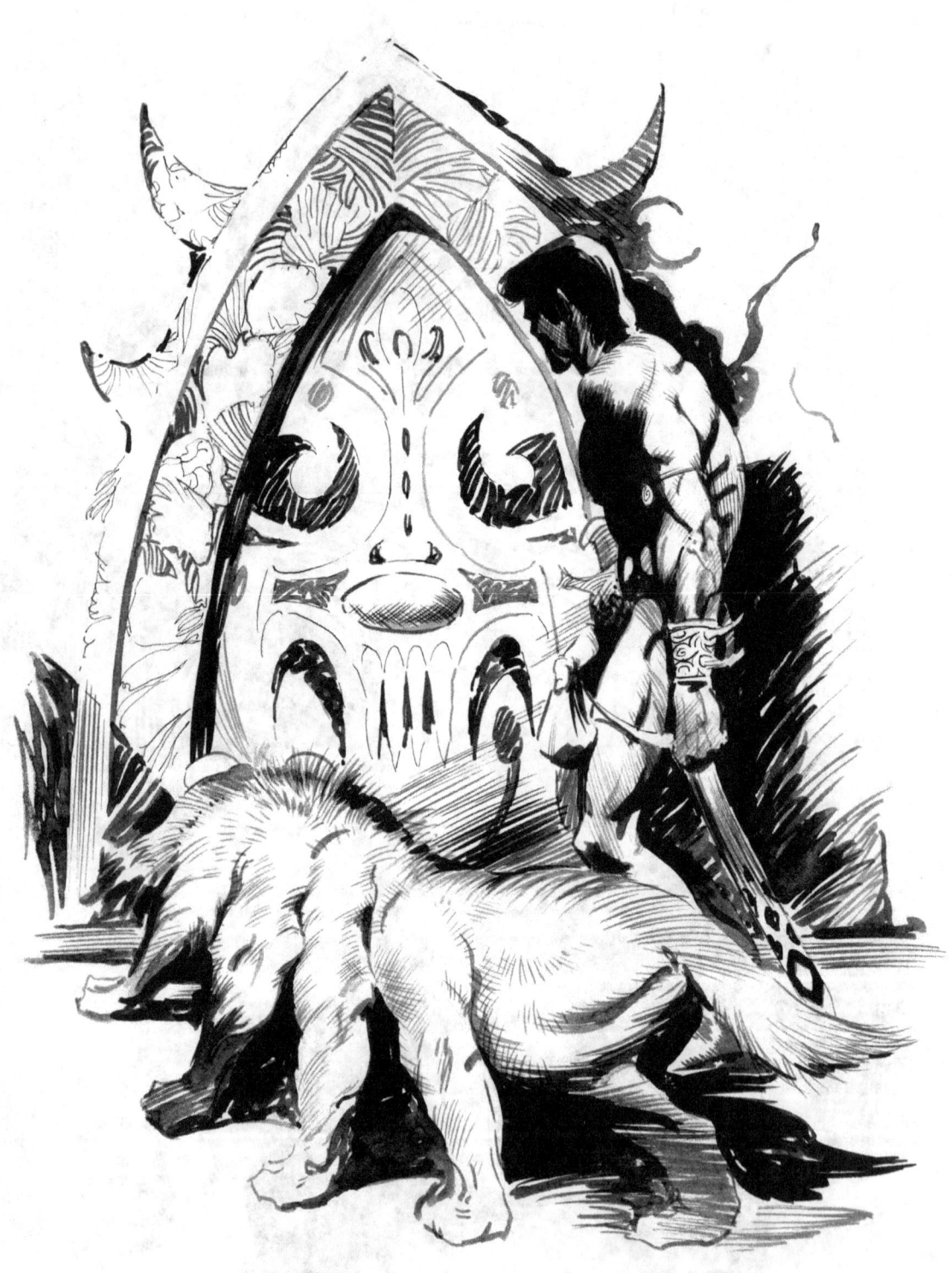

"I came suddenly upon the insignia
of the house of Thurid jewel-inset in
its metal case.I am upon the right"

"Clear to the hilt my weapon passed
through his body, and with a frightful
shriek he sank to the floor, dead."

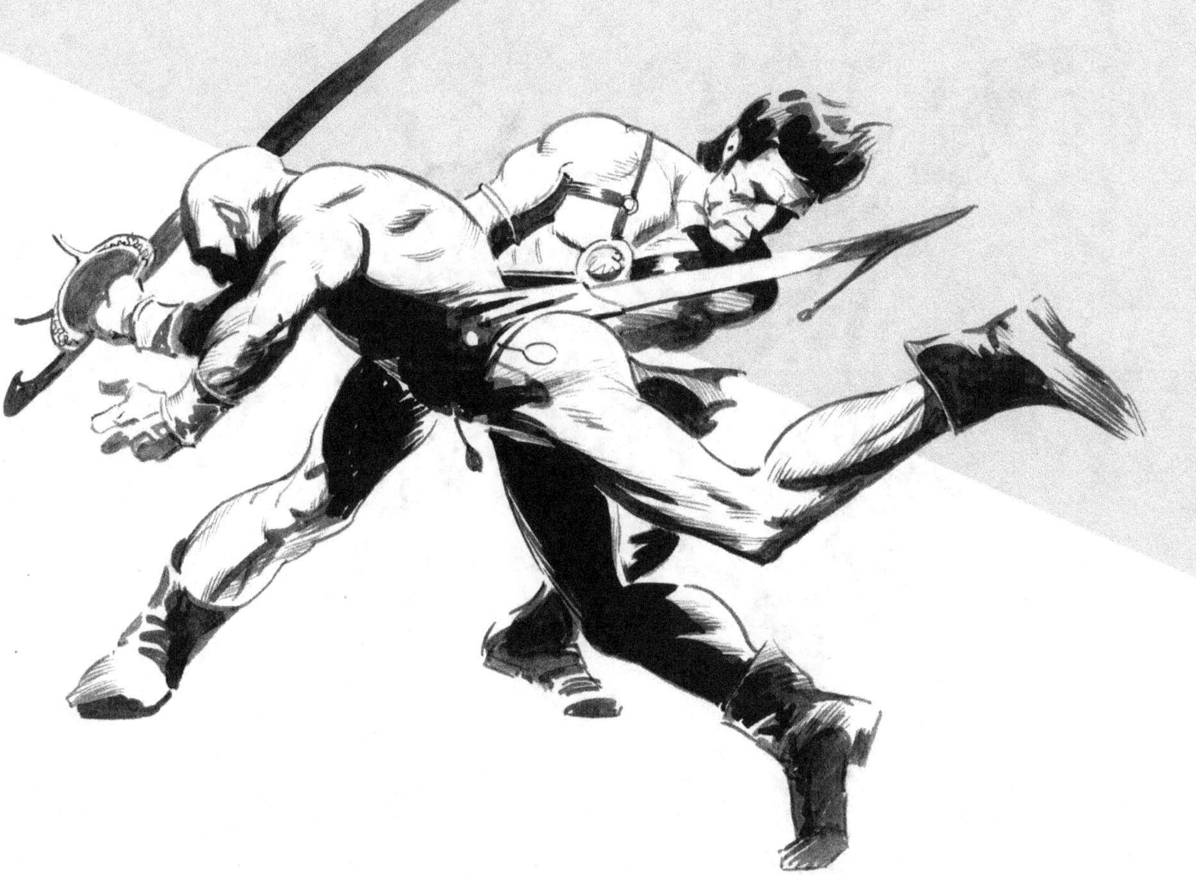

"...but presently their eyes, becoming accustomed
to the light, fell upon Woola and me, and with
bristling manes and deep-throated roars they
advanced..."

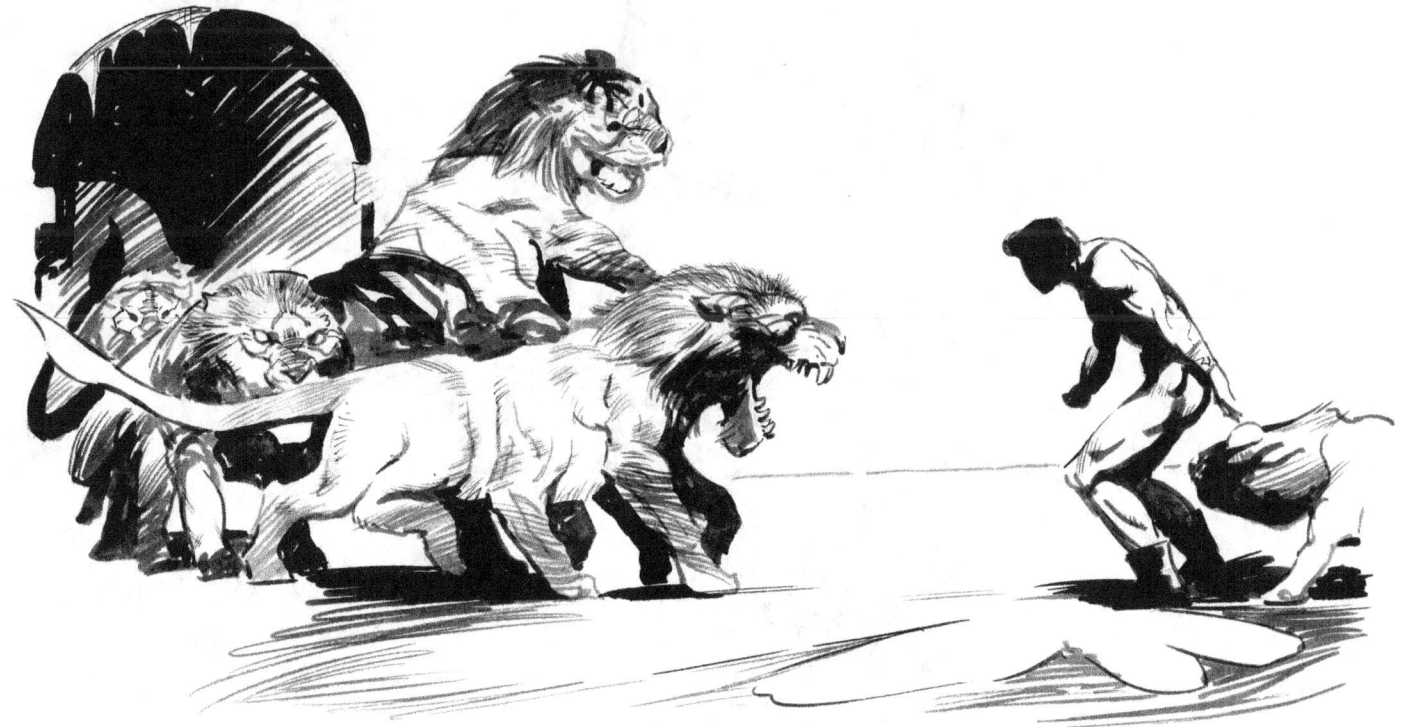

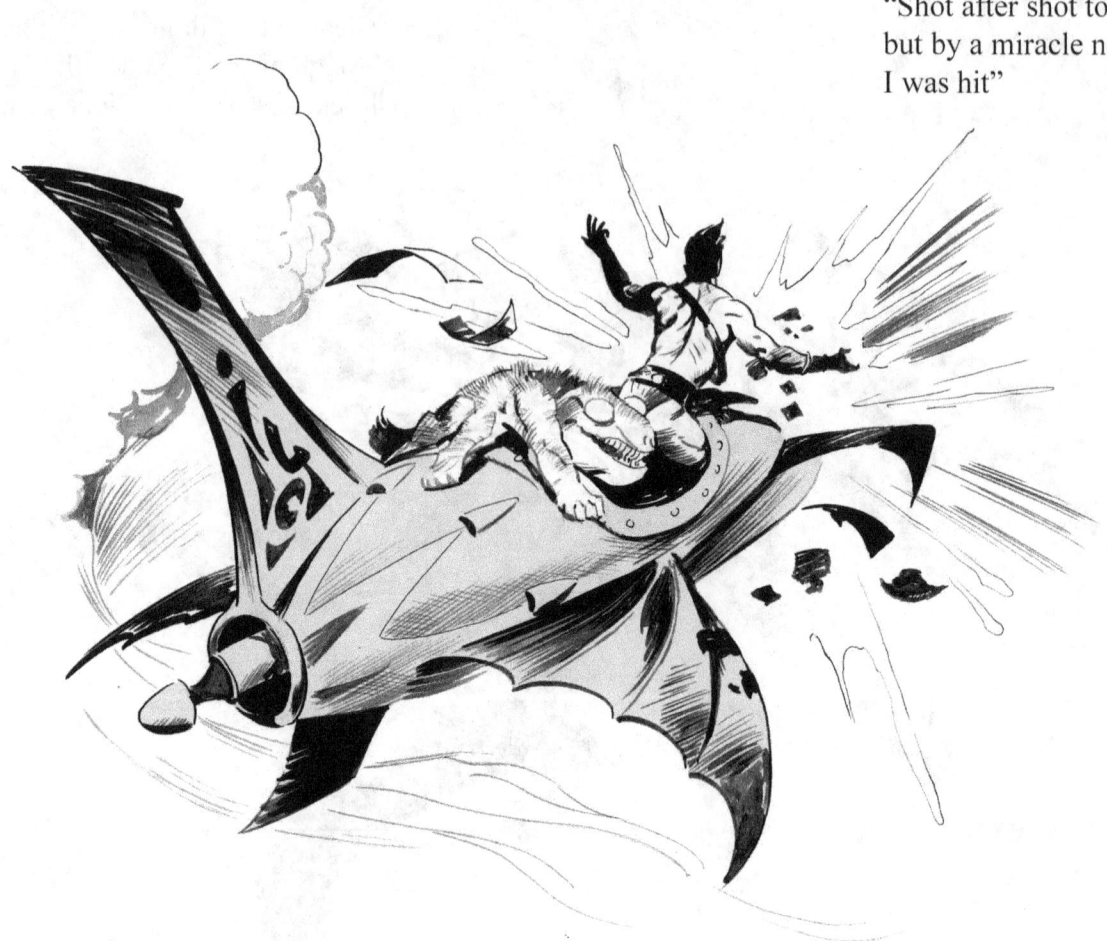

"Shot after shot tore past or into us, but by a miracle neither Woola nor I was hit"

"As Woola and I approached the bottom of the declivity the ground became soft and mushy, so that it was with the greatest difficulty that we made any headway whatever."

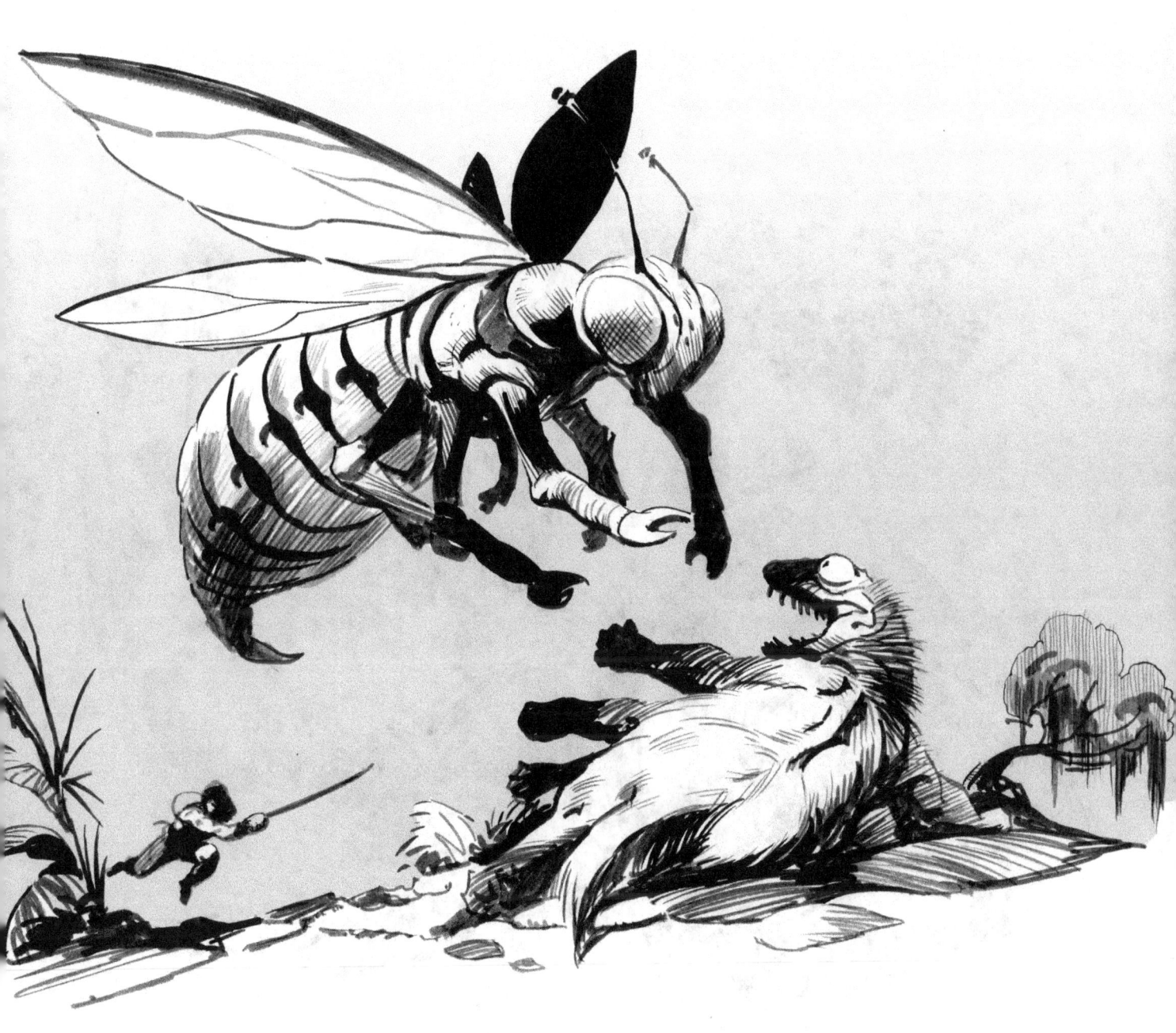

"Even my powerful and ferocious Woola
was as helpless as a kitten before that
frightful thing."

"...from behind the bole of a great tree I saw
a long line of the hideous green warriors..."

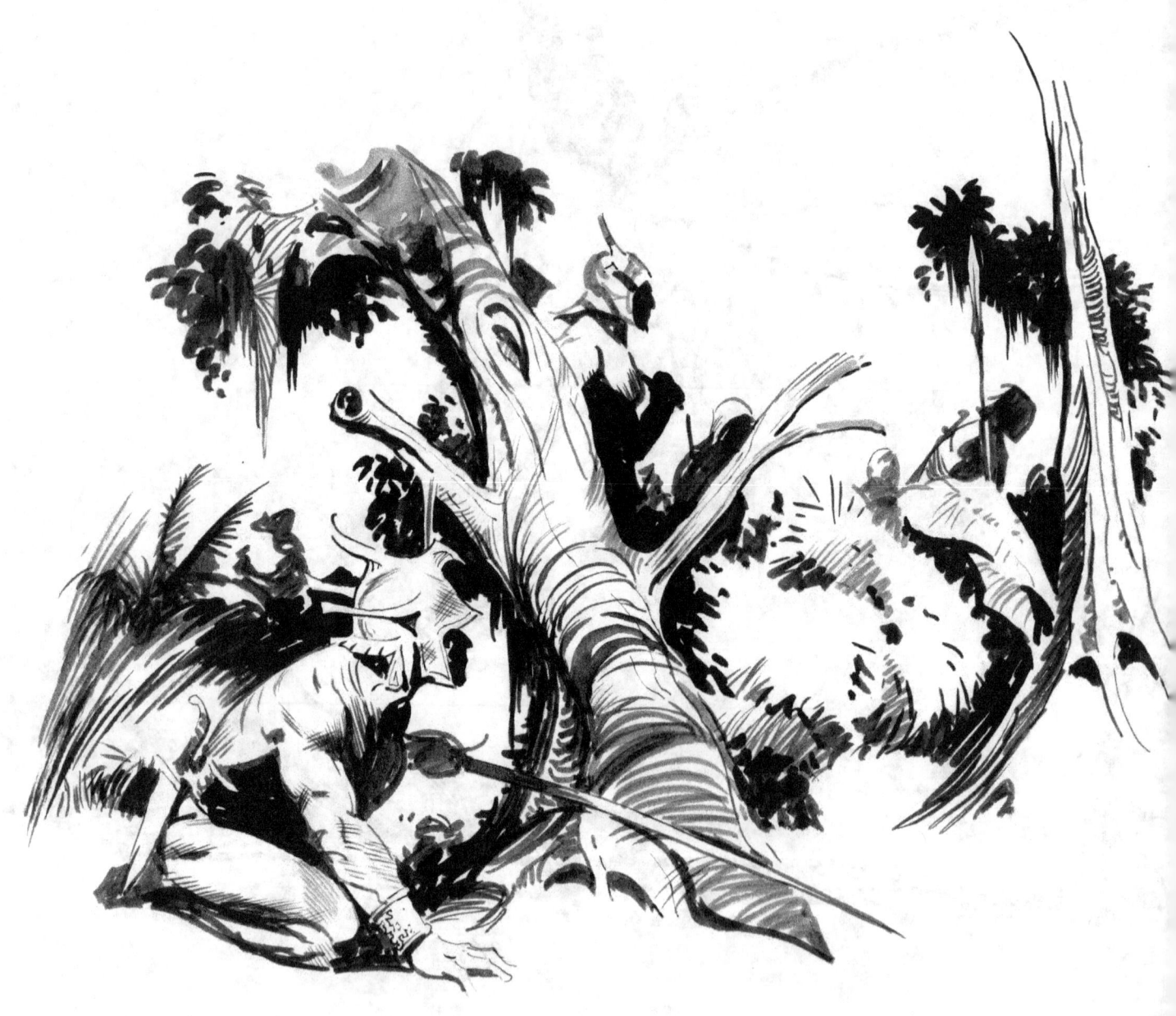

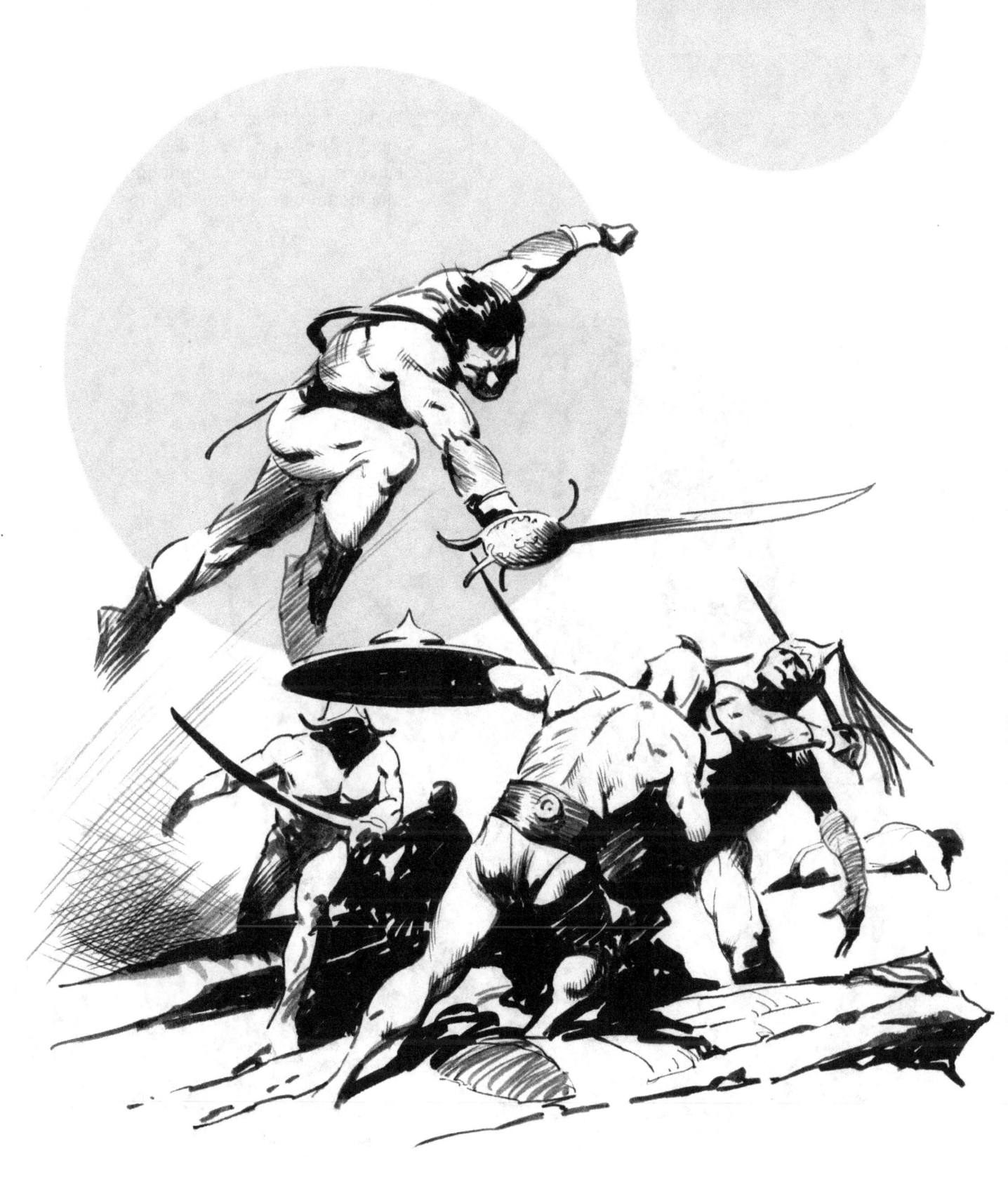

"...I leaped above their heads, and fashioning my tactics after those of the hideous plant men of Dor, struck down upon my enemies' heads as I passed above them."

"With a leap I was beside Thurid, and ere the devilish smirk had faded from his handsome face I had caught him full upon the mouth with my clenched fist..."

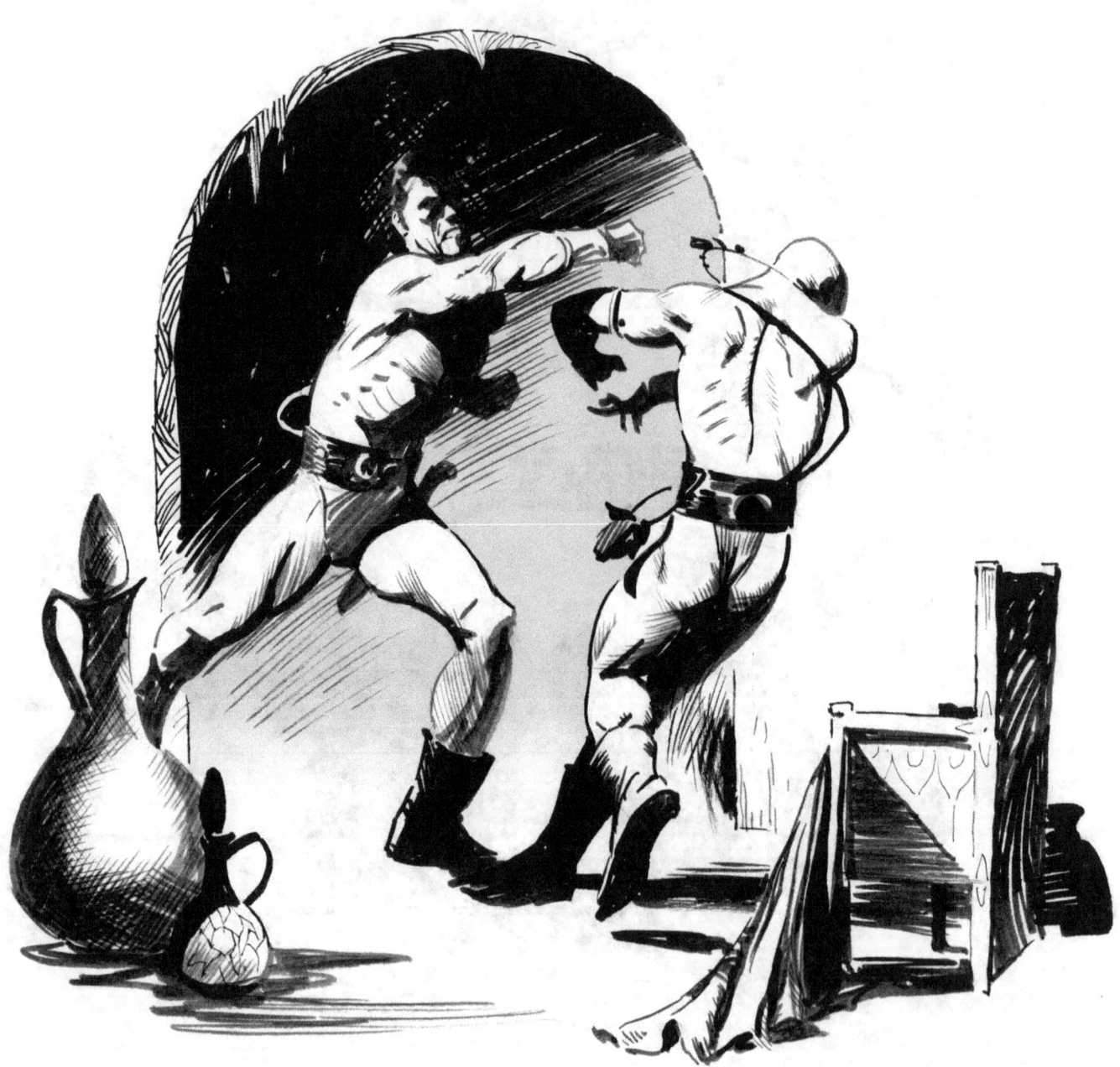

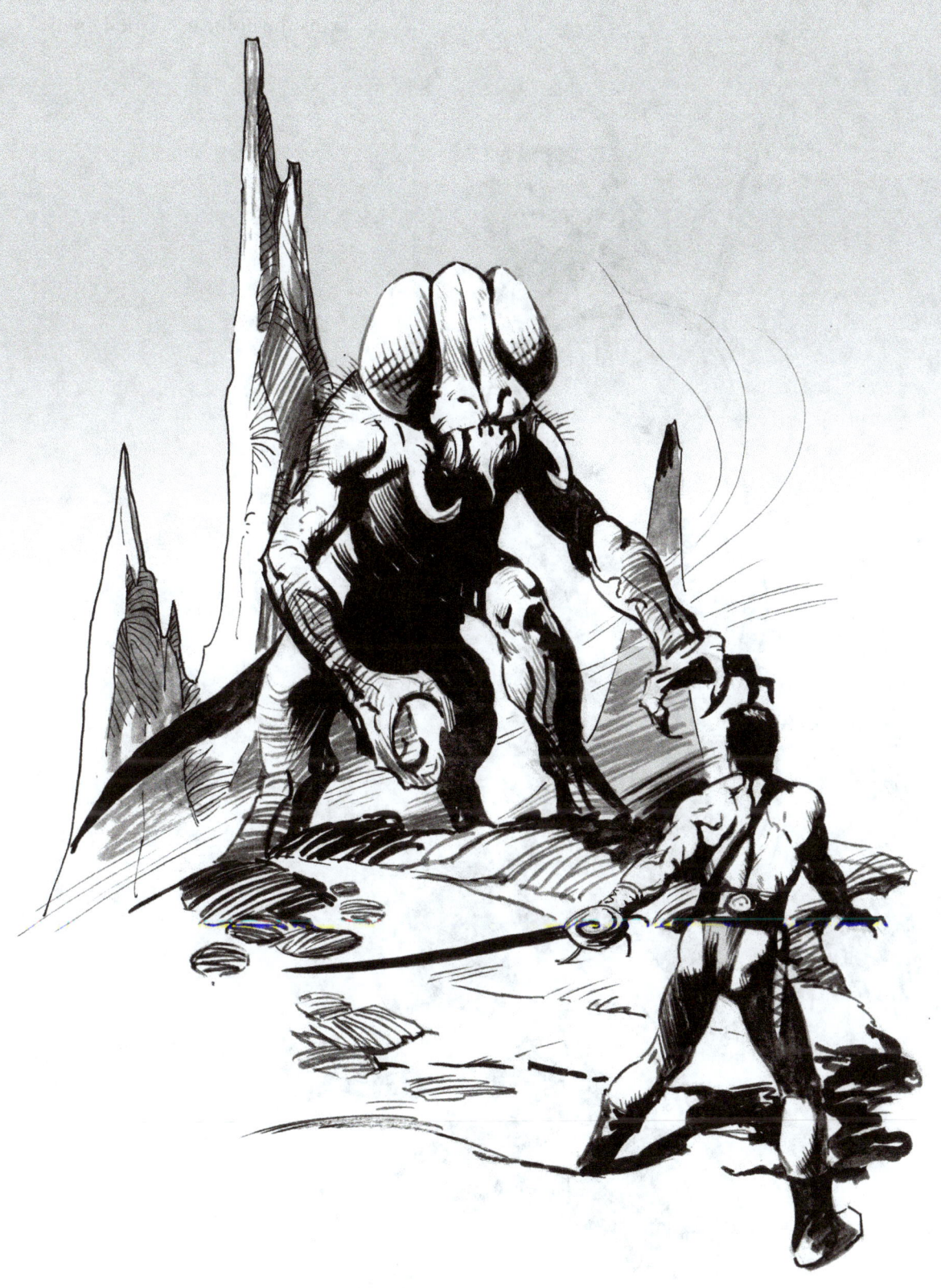

"The apt was our most consistent and dangerous foe."

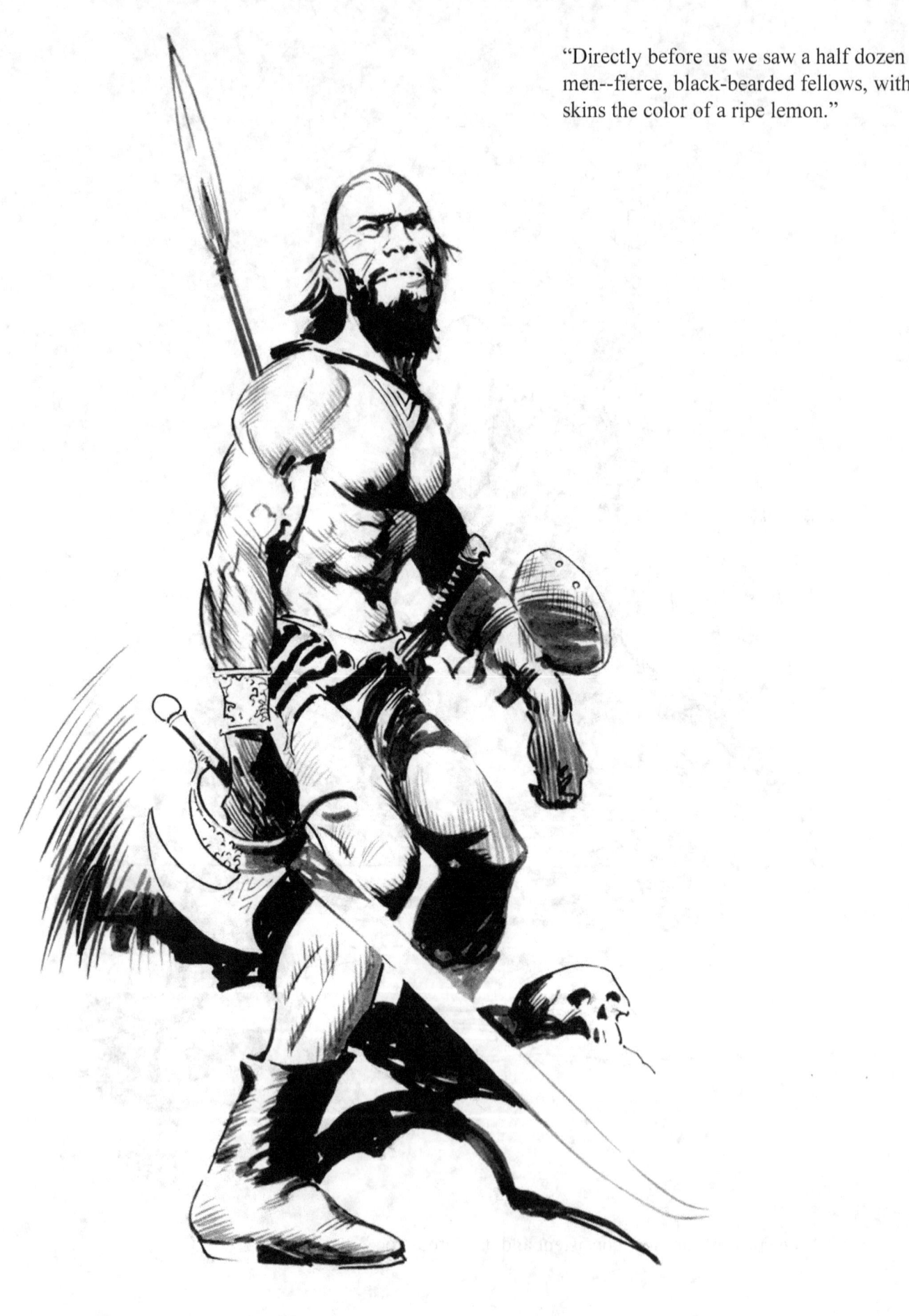

"Directly before us we saw a half dozen men--fierce, black-bearded fellows, with skins the color of a ripe lemon."

"At the same moment I recognized them--they were Dejah Thoris and Thuvia of Ptarth!"

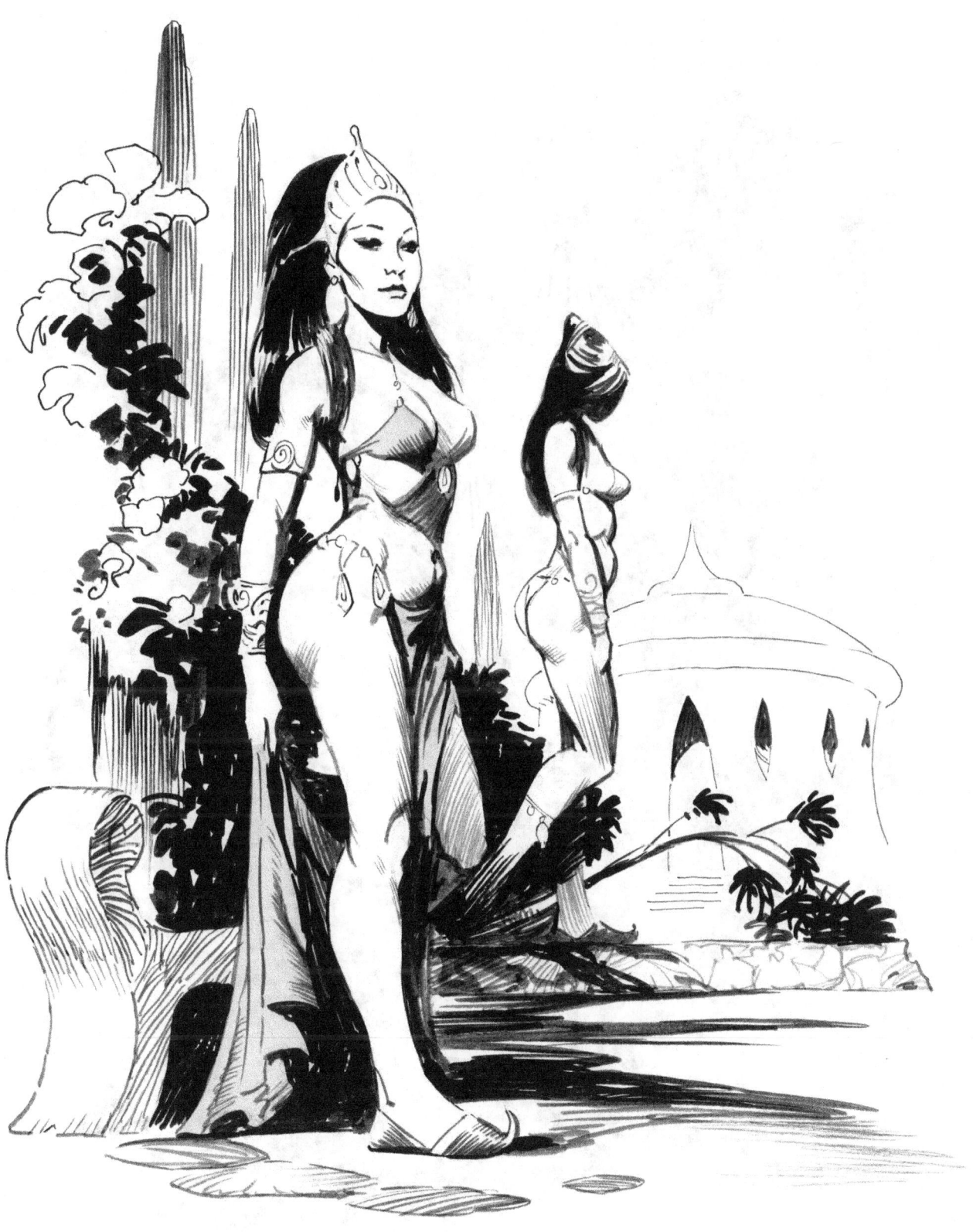

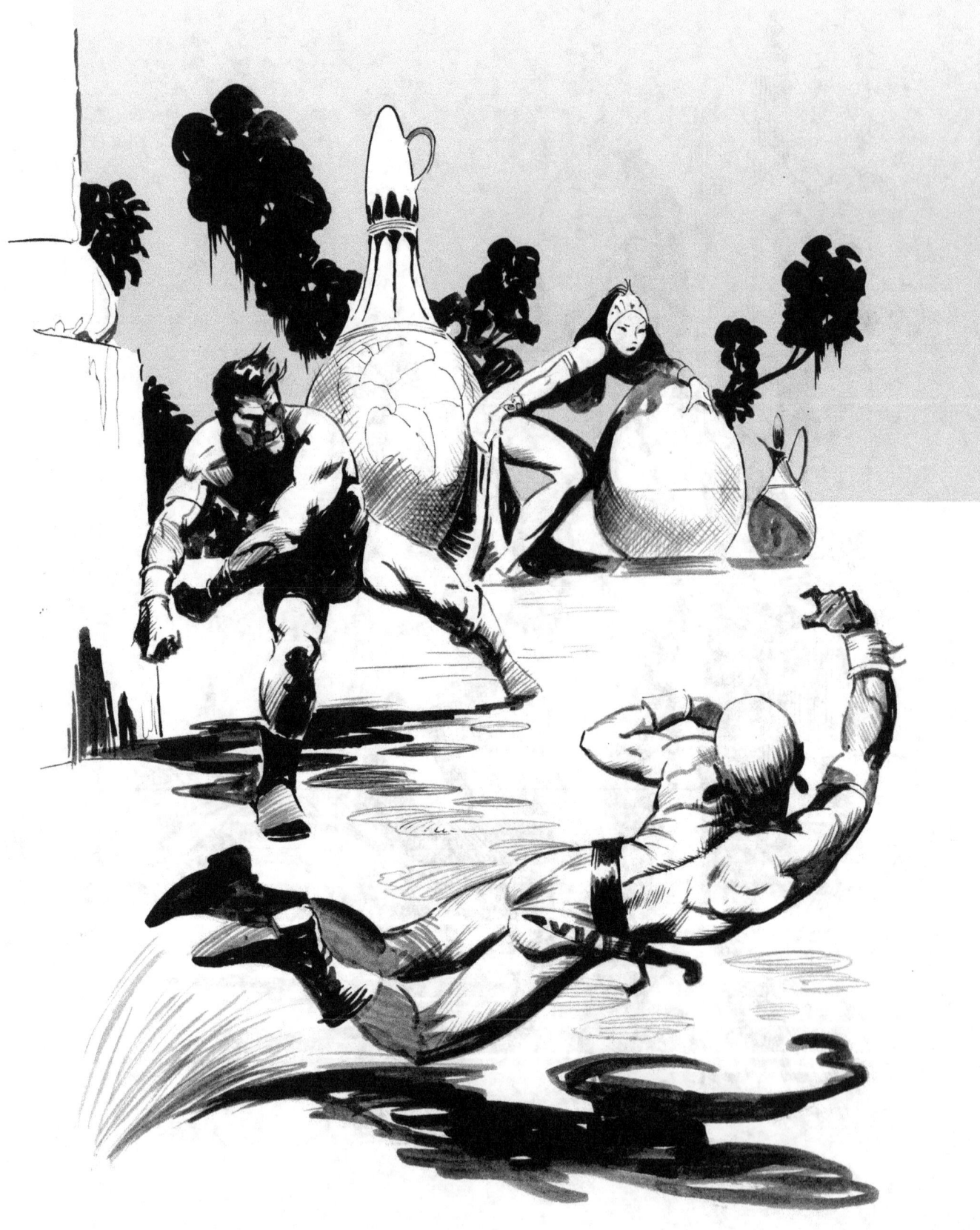

"I spoke no word as I tore his defiling fingers from that beautiful throat, nor did I utter a sound as I hurled him twenty feet from me."

"...on the instant that I saw her there, there sprang to my mind the firm intention never to leave that chamber alive if I must leave her in the clutches of this powerful tyrant."

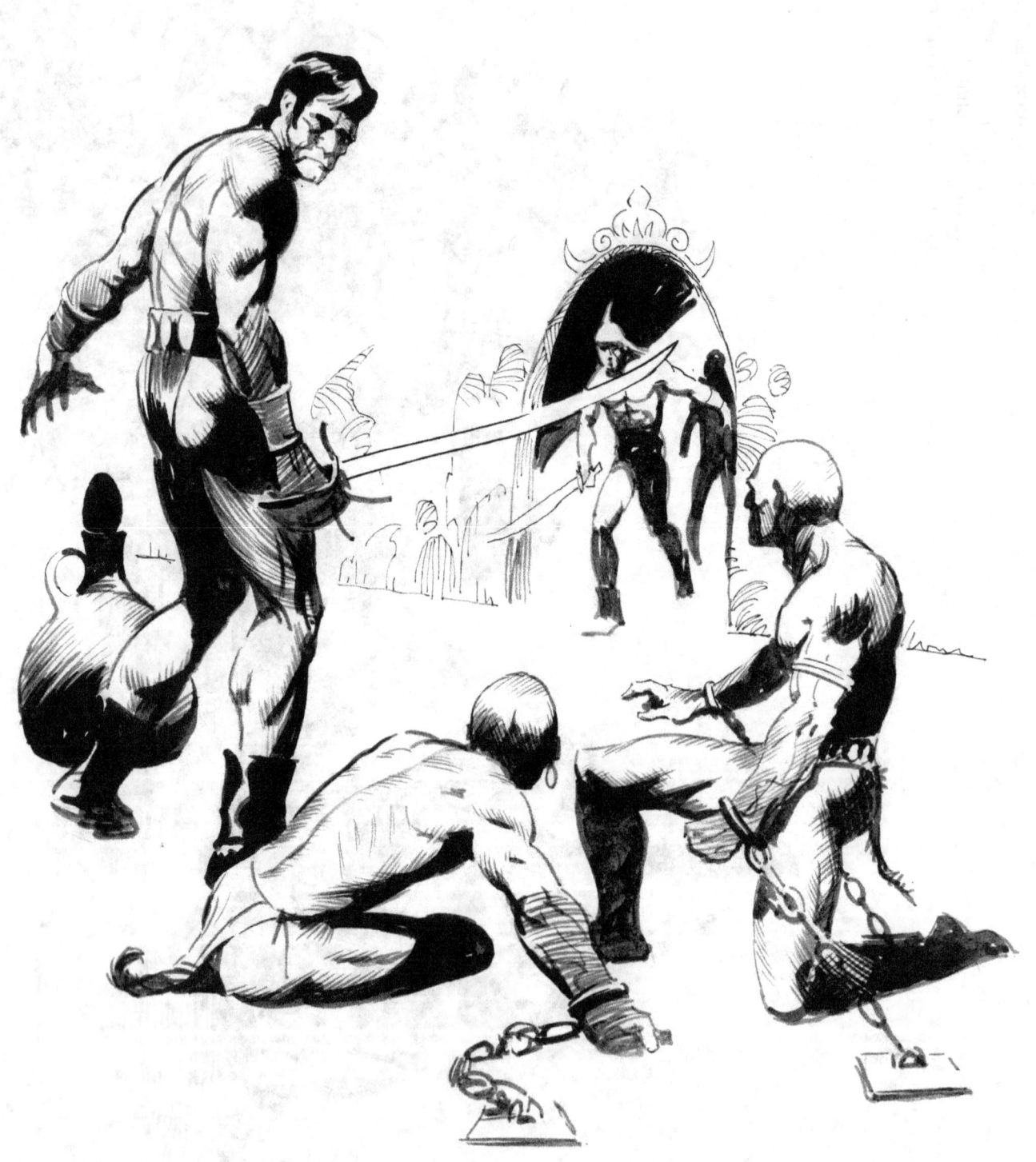

"...but scarce did we engage ere, to my horror,
I saw that the red slaves were shackled
to the floor."

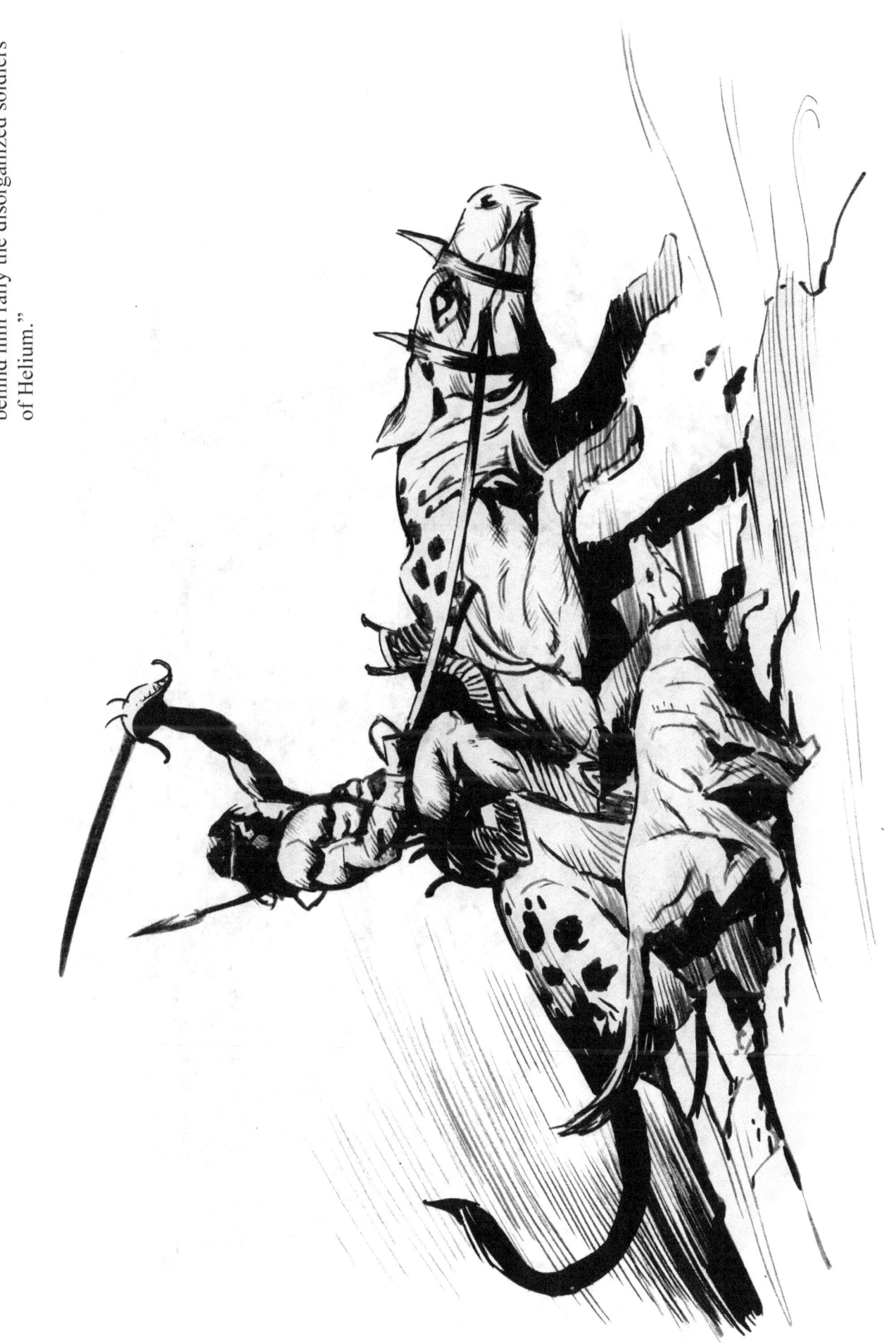

"The warrior hews his way to the front, and behind him rally the disorganized soldiers of Helium."

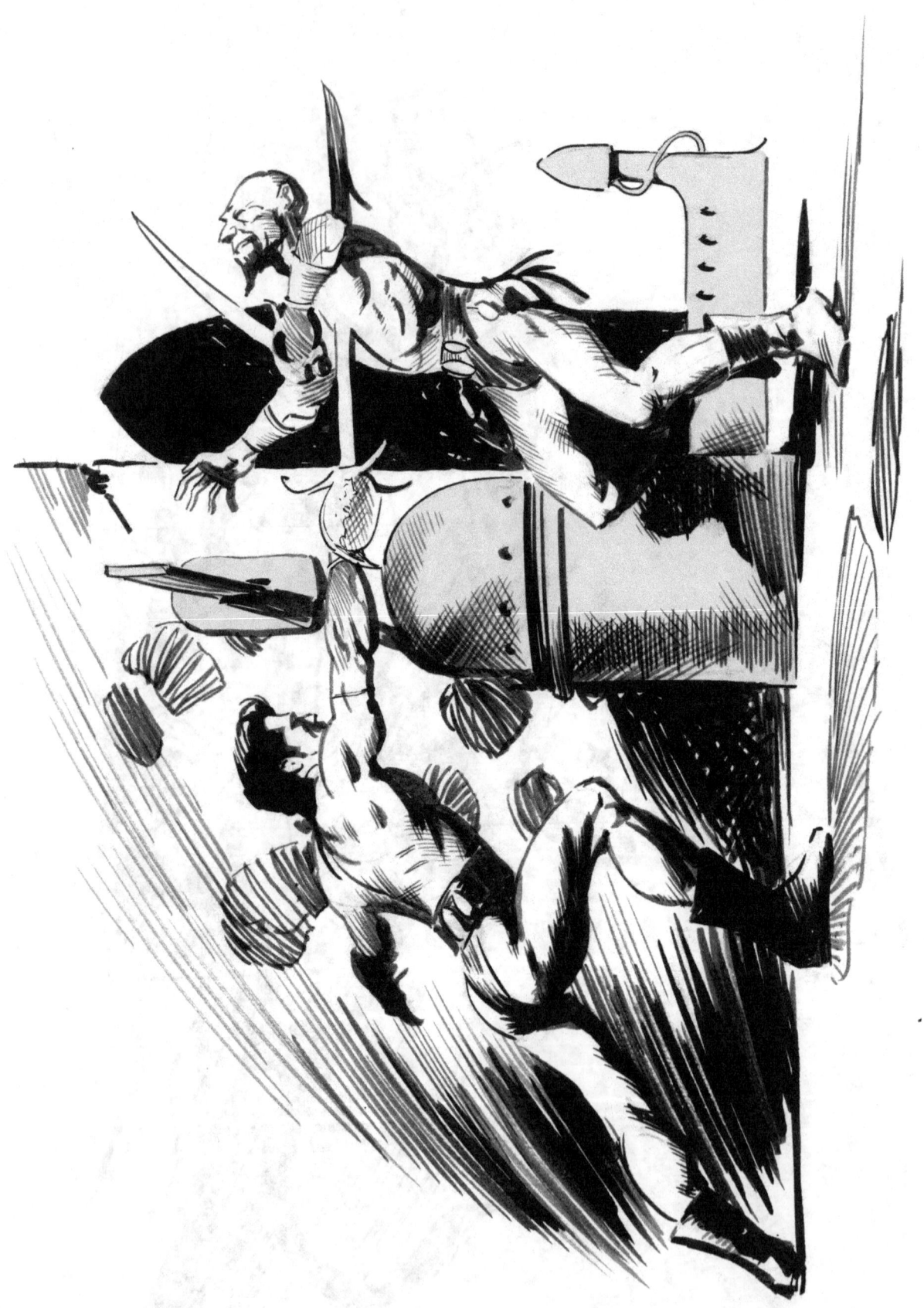

"...two guardsmen appeared dragging
the unwilling bride toward the altar."

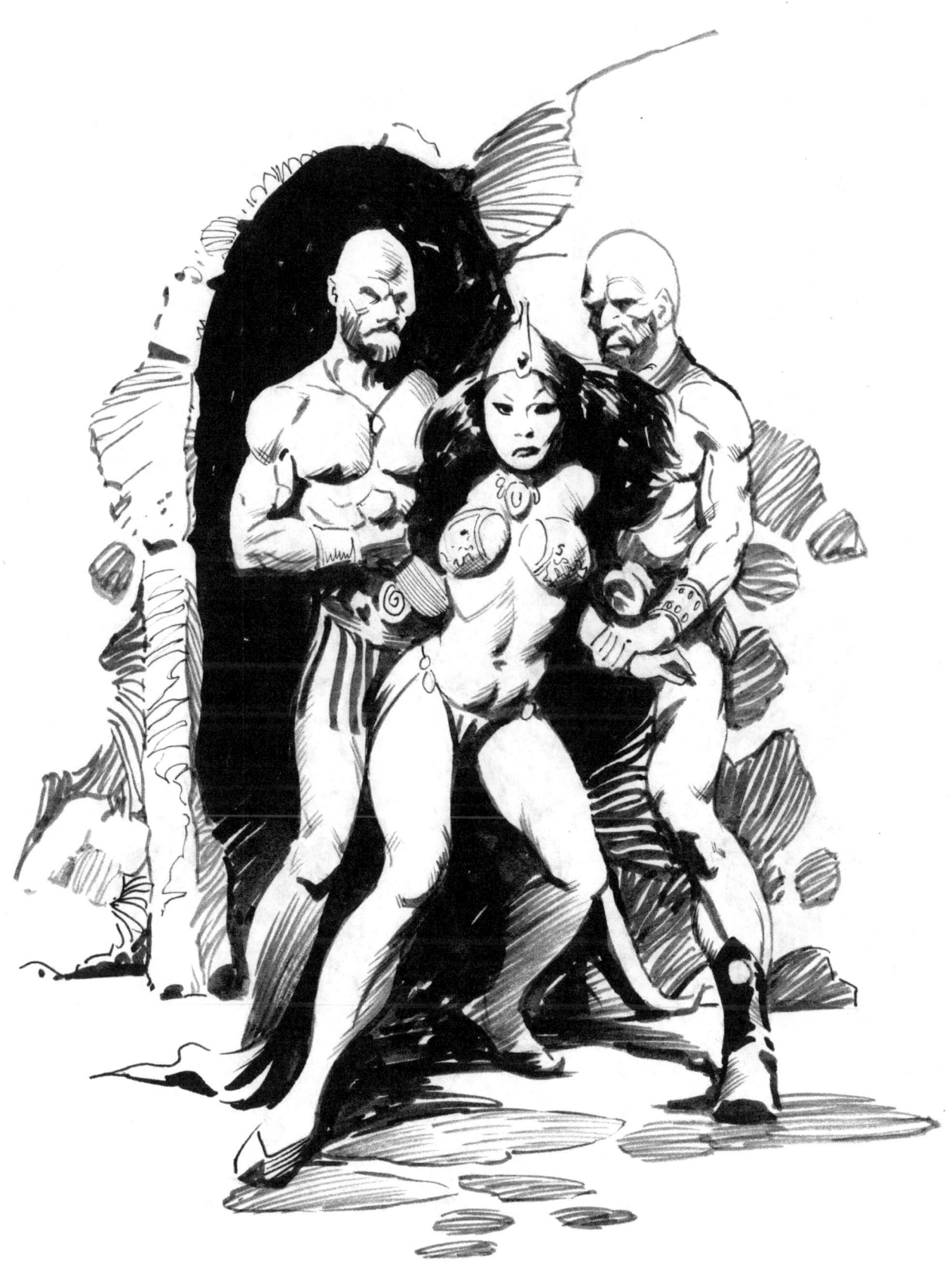

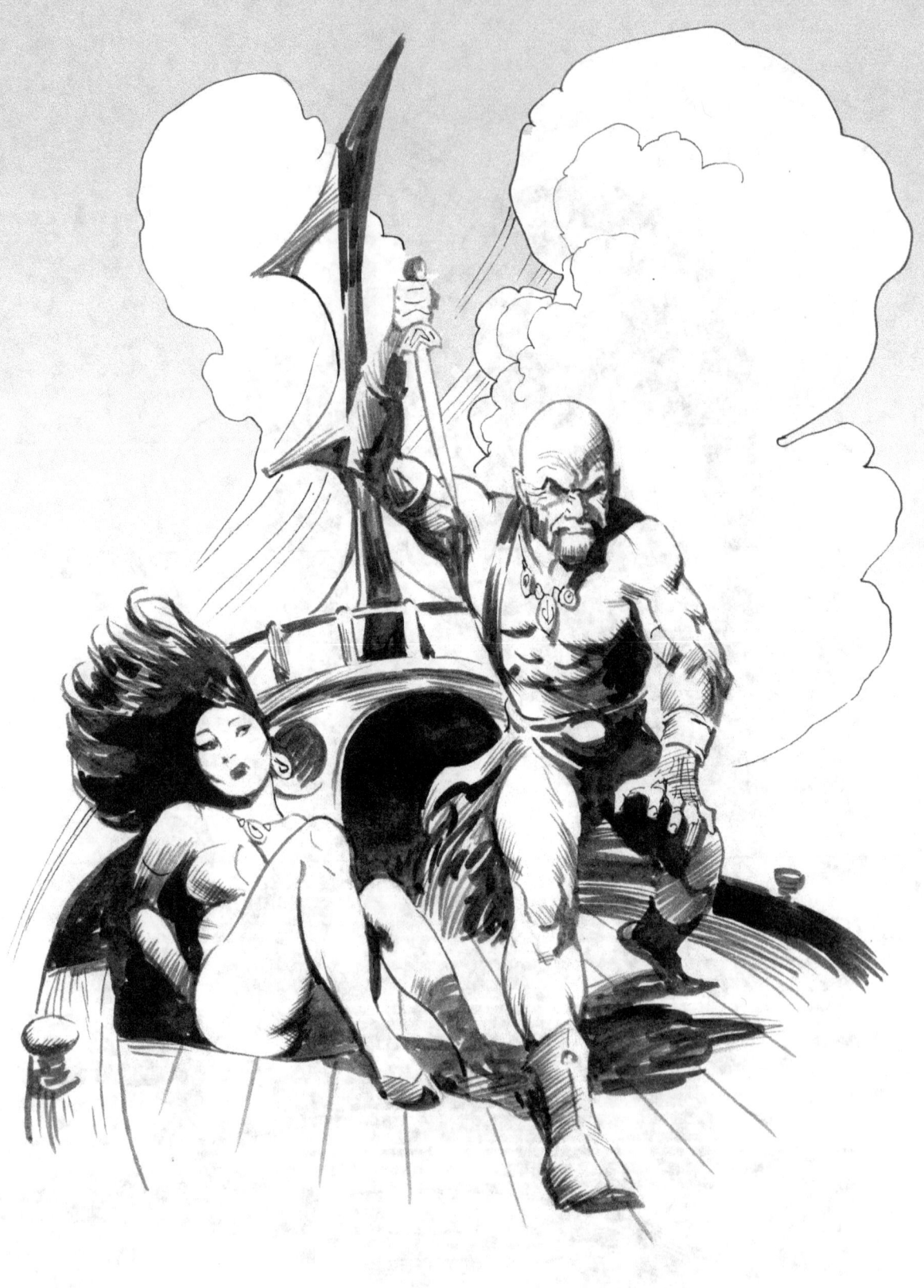

"Then my head came above the deck and
I saw Thurid, dagger in hand..."

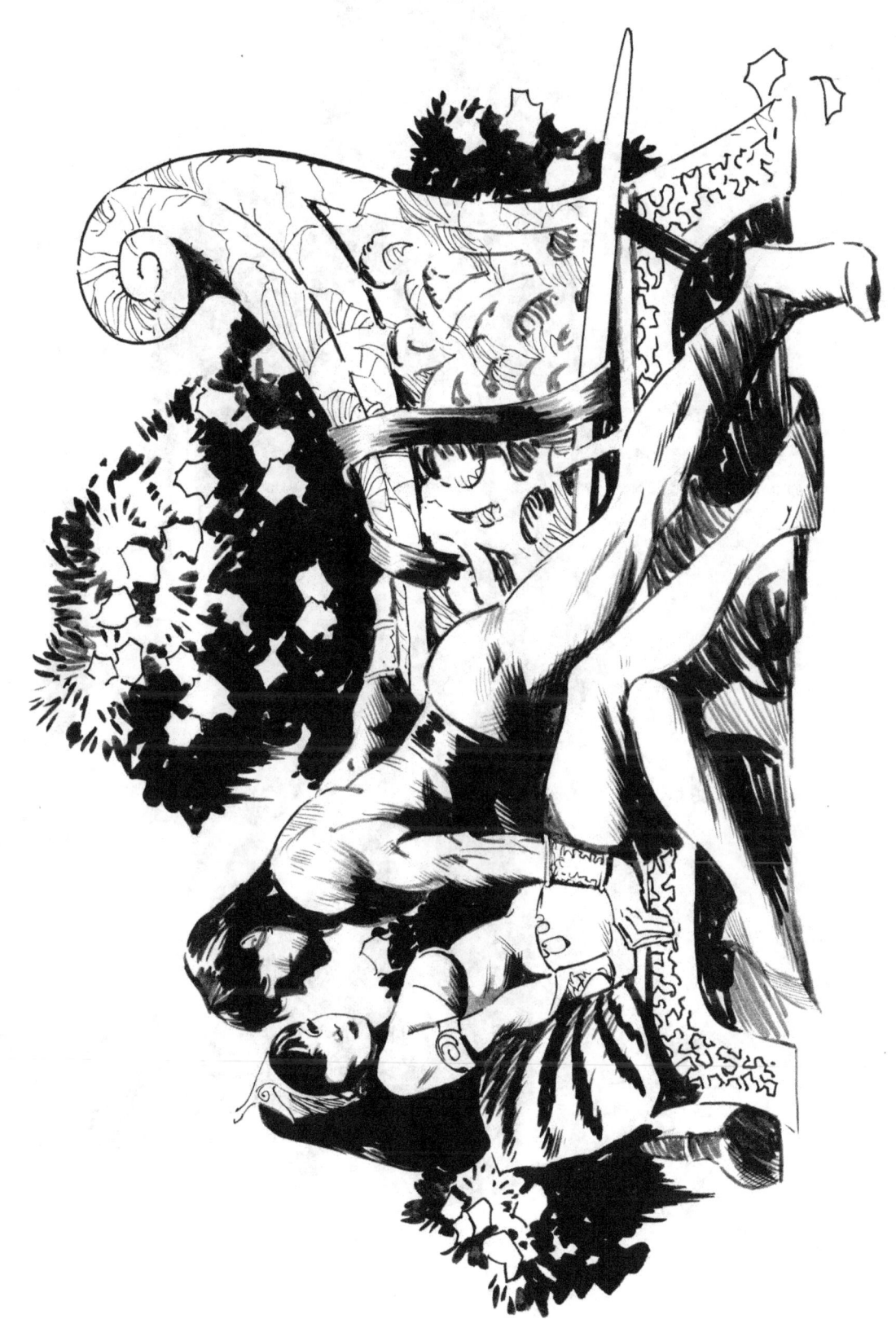

"The handsome head of the handsome youth was bent low above the beautiful face of his companion…"

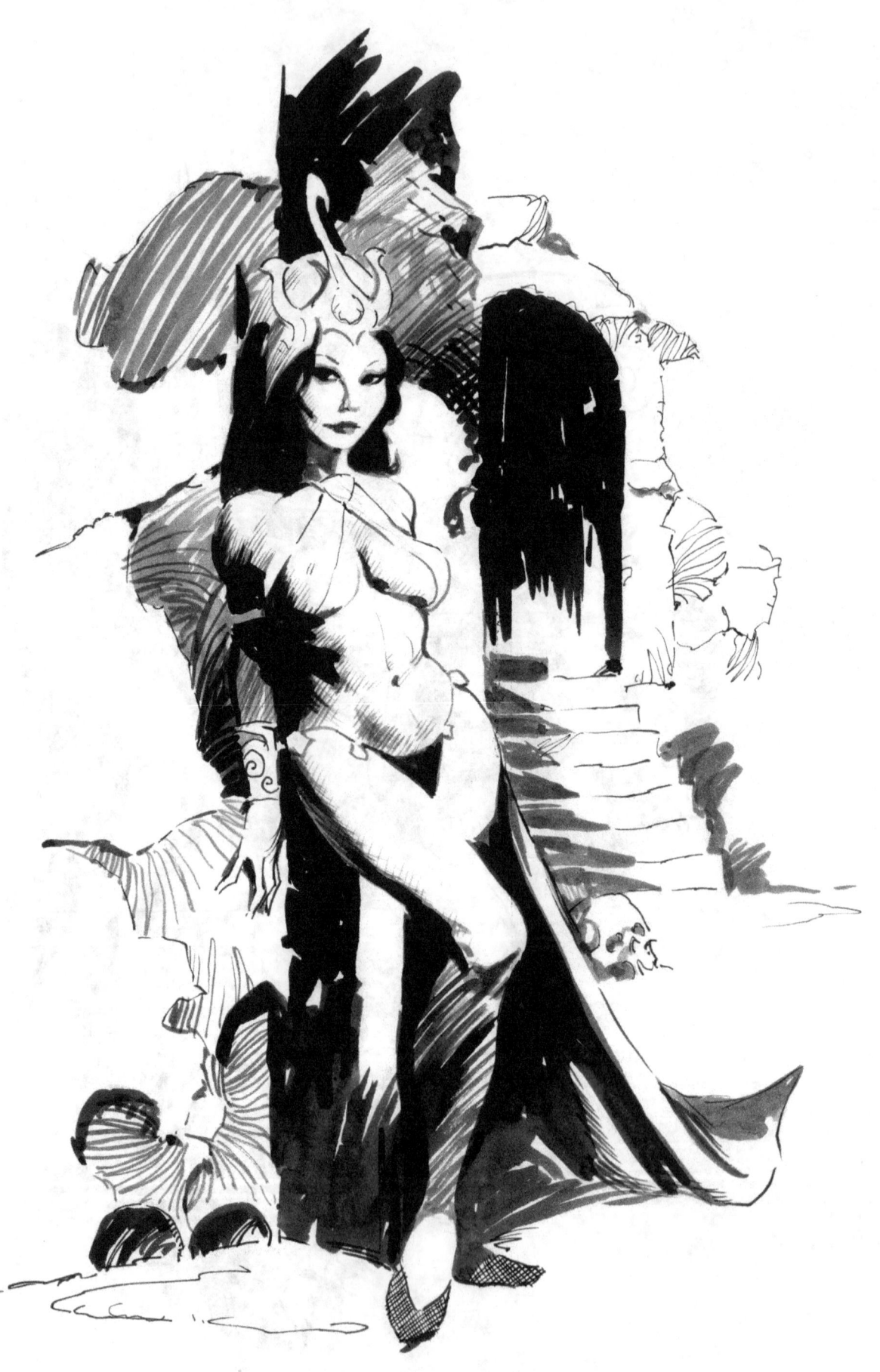

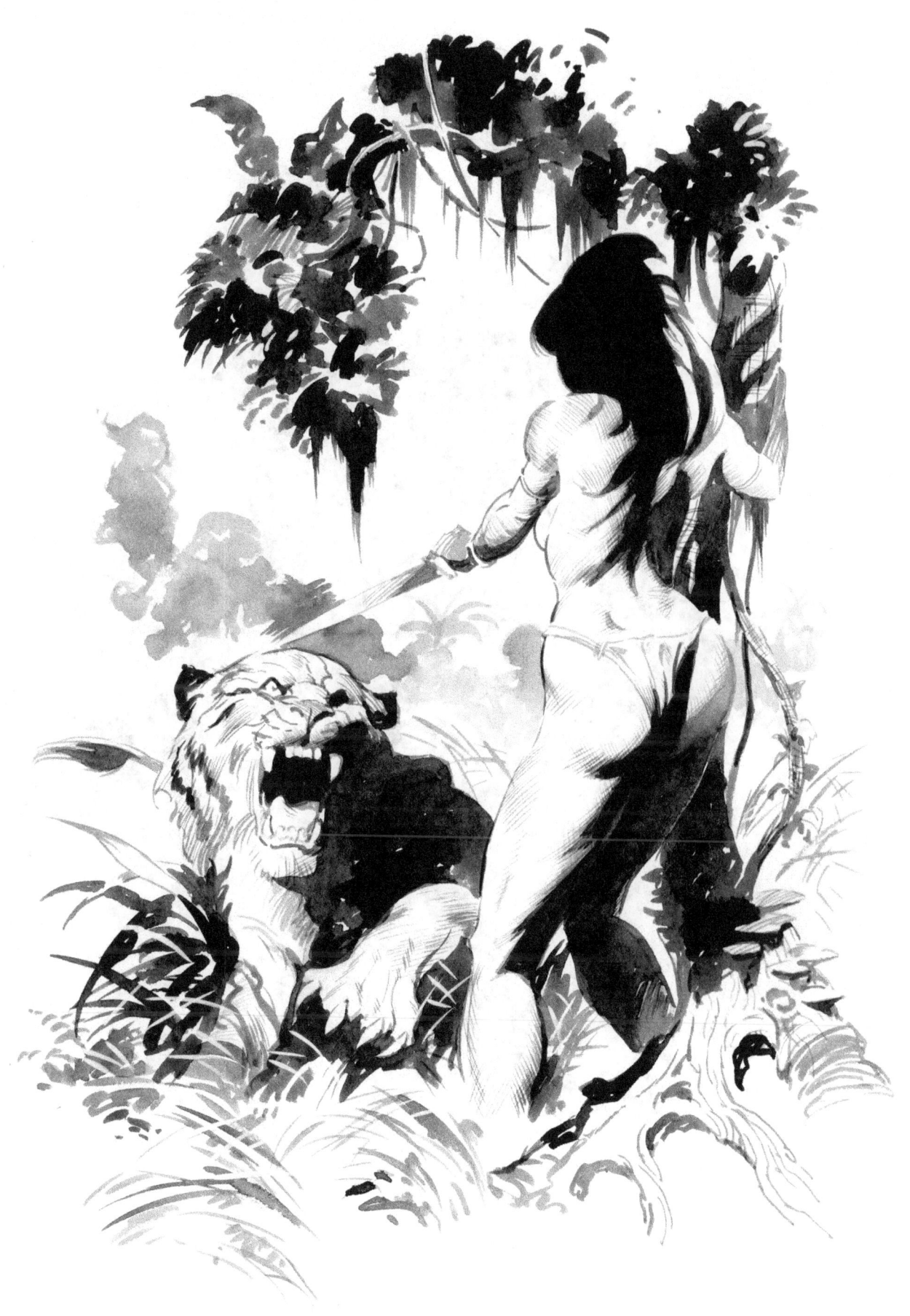

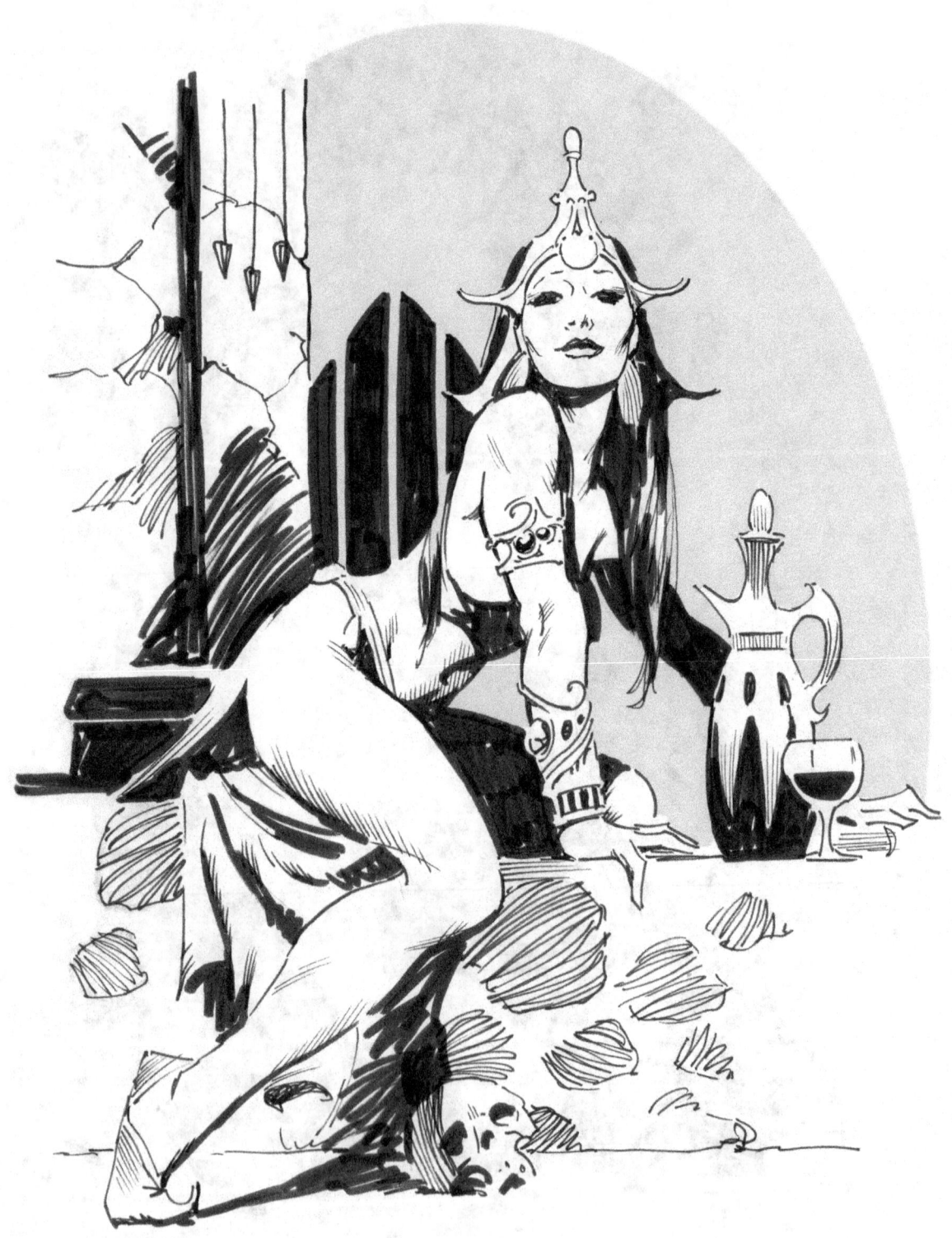

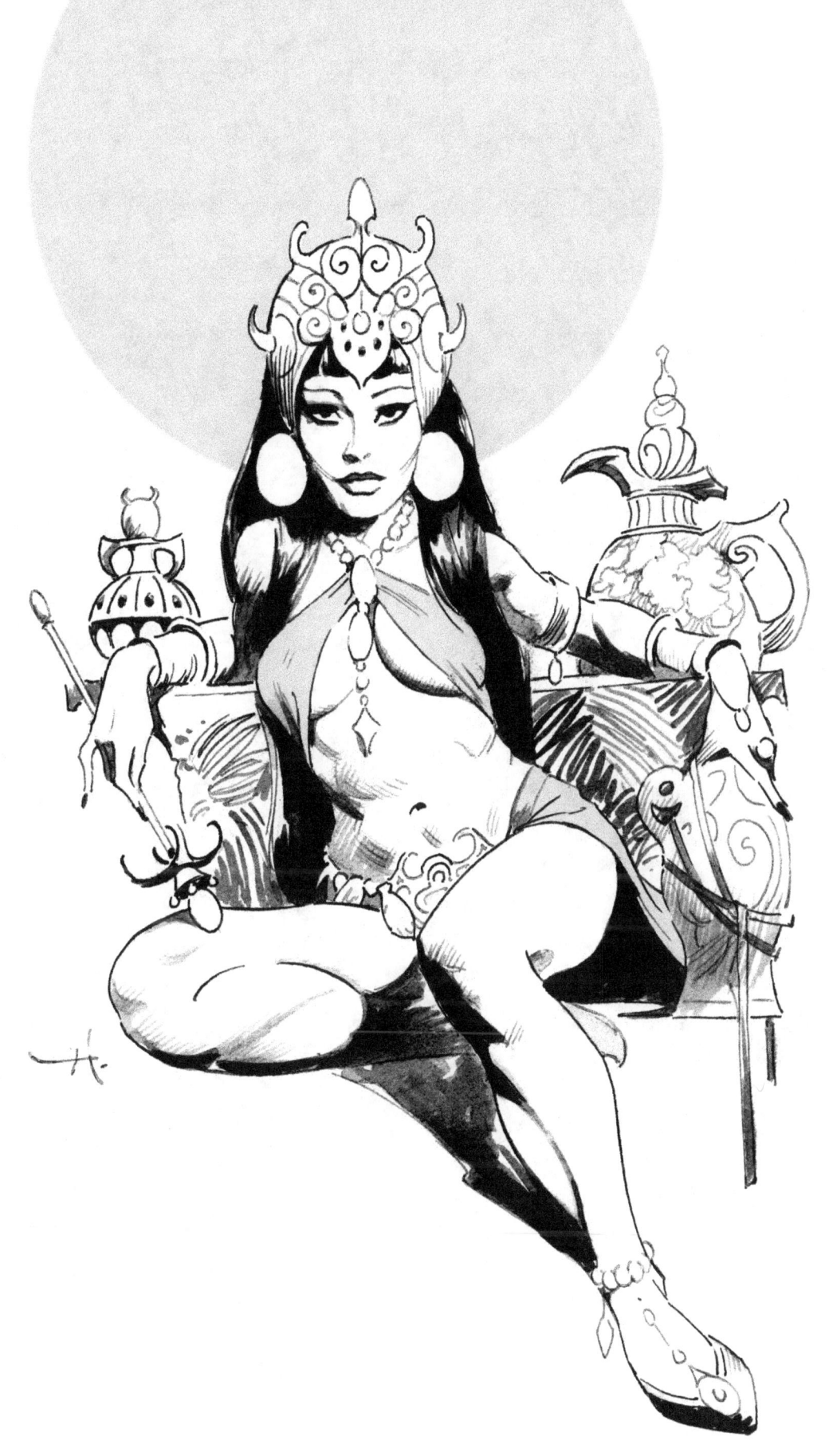